THREE PLAYS

**ISAAC SHEFTEL
THE LAST JEW
THE DUMB MESSIAH**

BY DAVID PINSKI
THE TREASURE
A DRAMA IN FOUR ACTS
ONE DOLLAR
NEW YORK: B. W. HUEBSCH

THREE PLAYS

BY
DAVID PINSKI

AUTHORIZED TRANSLATION FROM THE YIDDISH BY
ISAAC GOLDBERG

NEW YORK
B. W. HUEBSCH
MCMXVIII

COPYRIGHT, 1918, BY
B. W. HUEBSCH

PRINTED IN U. S. A.

INTRODUCTION

The twenty-seven plays thus far written by David Pinski may be grouped according to several distinct manners which the playwright has developed. Earliest to appear, as a natural offspring of the proletarian tales that first brought him fame as the discoverer of the Jewish working class, was the drama depicting life among humble folk. The outstanding example of this style is *Isaac Sheftel*, 1899. With *The Last Jew* (*Die Familie Zwie*), 1903-4, Pinski rose from his people's sufferings to the vision of their redemption and the psychological reaction of that vision. This phase of his work came to full fruition in *The Dumb Messiah*, 1911. In one of the greatest plays written in the twentieth century, *The Treasure*, 1906, the dramatist glorified the symbolism and satire already evident in *The Last Jew*, producing a bitter comedy that was to have its less acrid sequel in the purely symbolic, optimistic *Mountain Climbers*, 1912. *Jacob the Blacksmith*, 1906, and notably *Gabriel and the Women*, 1908, initiate the full-length treatment of love and the contemporary sex-problem that had been forecasted in the one-act masterpiece, *Forgotten Souls*, 1904, the most recent examples being the brutally realistic *Better Unborn*, 1914, and the remarkably concise, penetrating *Nina Marden's Loves*, 1915–16. Pinski's purely biblical manner, as distinct from the Messianic dramas mentioned above, is most strikingly illustrated by a series of five one-act plays written between 1913 and 1915, *King David and his Wives*.

It would be inexact to designate these various manners as "periods" in the progress of the playwright. They do not follow one another in chronological sequence; once, indeed, in a single year, 1906, three manners appear in rapid succession. Again, whatever Pinski writes possesses a vital contemporary significance, so that even his biblical plays, though ancient in inspiration, are distinctly modern in meaning. Yet again, some plays reveal a blending of styles; *Mary Magdalene*, 1910, for instance, belongs at once to the playwright's biblical and sex-problem categories.

When we consider what a relatively large number of Pinski's plays dispense entirely with the love interest and in how many others it is a secondary element — true, too, of his tales — we come to a realization of his chief significance to the contemporary drama. Pinski is, first of all, a realistic psychologist. His portrait gallery is a notable collection of seekers, of souls that have lusted for power and found themselves beaten by powers greater than their own. Death, suicide or resignation is the common lot of such seekers.

Tille, Mary, Gail, Nina Marden,— all are spiritual sisters who seek, by divers means, to achieve dominance. Tille (*The Treasure*) purchases it for a day by a lie that upsets the entire community and exposes the hypocrisy that hides beneath religious garb. Mary of Magdala would triumph over Christ by the sheer voluptuousness of her beauty, yet succumbs to a higher beauty. Gail (*Gabriel and the Women*) conquers her wayward husband through patience and the more homely virtues of womankind; she is a modern Griselda. For Nina Marden is reserved the fate of corrupting every man she seeks to inspire; she would employ her beauty to call forth the best in man, yet can bring out only the worst.

INTRODUCTION   vii

So, too, with Pinski's male protagonists. Isaac Sheftel's intense will to be and to do crumbles upon the ruins of his scant foundations. His is the tragedy of creative vision balked by limitations of environment and education. Reb Mayshe, also (*The Last Jew*), falls upon the threshold of a vision never to be seen by his eyes. The soul of the obsessed Menahem Penini (*The Dumb Messiah*) founders likewise upon the rock of disillusionment.

The plays chosen for inclusion in this volume are arranged in chronological order.

Isaac Sheftel was written from the twenty-first of March to the seventh of April, 1899, in Berlin. The actual time spent upon composition was thirteen days, the last act having been written in seven hours, without interruption. The chief character was suggested to the dramatist by the strange figure of a Warsaw workingman who was gifted with inventive talent, yet sold his contrivances to his employer for a mere pittance in order always to be near his beloved brain children.

The Last Jew, known in Yiddish and in other tongues as The Zwie Family, was first conceived in 1900, but only after the Kishinev anti-Semite massacre did the background and the action suggest themselves. The first two acts were written in the summer of 1903; the third act was composed on the twentieth of May, 1904, the day of an examination at Columbia University where Pinski was a post-graduate student, which would have led to his degree as Doctor of Philosophy. The fourth act was completed soon after the third, in two or three days.

Peculiar historic interest is attached to the tragedy. It has been given wherever there were enough Jews to organize a small theater; the one exception to this is New York, where it has never been given in Yiddish upon the legitimate stage, although the well-known Russian actor, Orlenev, produced it there in Russian in 1905-6. Until the period of the first revolution it was forbidden in Russia; for a while after the revolution its presentation was permitted, but in Yiddish only. The tragedy was printed on the thinnest paper, sewed into coats and smuggled into Russia. Secret societies (whence originated the Yiddish amateur stage) sprang up for the purpose of producing the forbidden play. One of these companies was caught red-handed by the government; so effective was the punishment that further production was stifled. This official persecution followed the play to the Moscow Art Theater, where the noted director, Stanislavski, was to produce it in 1907. The censor interdicted the Russian version.

The play has been given in Berlin, at the Schiller Theater, in a German translation. It has been translated into Hebrew, and in the Yiddish original has already gone through thirteen editions.

The Dumb Messiah was composed in four days, from the twenty-ninth of July to the third of August, 1911. It followed fast upon *Professor Brenner* (a beautiful study of a mature intellect wedded to a youthful beauty) and was written in that feverish glow that attends the writing of so many of Pinski's pieces. He began without a clear conception of the action or of even the minor characters. Thus, the figures of Blanche the Beggar and Leah came into being after the work was begun.

Isaac Goldberg.

Roxbury, Mass., March, 1918.

CONTENTS

	PAGE
INTRODUCTION BY THE TRANSLATOR	v
ISAAC SHEFTEL	1
THE LAST JEW [DIE FAMILIE ZWIE]	81
THE DUMB MESSIAH	167

CHRONOLOGICAL LIST OF DAVID PINSKI'S PLAYS

Sufferings *	1899	The Mountain Climbers ‡	1912
Isaac Sheftel †	1899	To Each Man His Own God ‡	1912
The Mother †	1901		
The Last Jew (*Die Familie Zwie*) ‡	1903–4	Bathsheba *	1913
Forgotten Souls *	1904	Conscience *	1913
The Eternal Jew *	1906	A Dollar! *	1913
The Treasure ‡	1906	Michal *	1914
Jacob the Blacksmith ‡	1906	Abigail *	1914
		In the Harem *	1914
Gabriel and the Women †	1908	Better Unborn ‡	1914
With Banners of Victory *	1908	Abishag *	1915
		Diplomacy *	1915
Mary Magdalene †	1910	Nina Marden's Loves ‡	1915–16
Professor Brenner †	1911		
The Dumb Messiah †	1911	Little Heroes *	1916
The Phonograph *	1918		

Bathsheba, Michal, Abigail, In the Harem and *Abishag* are grouped together under the title *King David and his Wives.*

* One act.   † Three acts.   ‡ Four acts.

ISAAC SHEFTEL

A DRAMA IN THREE ACTS
[1899]

PERSONS OF THE DRAMA

ISAAC SHEFTEL, *a lace-maker.*

BAYLYE, *his wife.*

GISHINKE,
ELINKE, } *their children.*

PINYE, *Isaac's feeble-minded father.*

NOTTE GOLDIN, *Isaac's employer.*

ORKE GOLDIN, *his son.*

OLD MICHEL,
RED BERRE,
FUNNY ZELIG,
LEIVIK, } *Workingmen in Goldin's factory.*
SENDER,
HILYE,
YOSHKE,

TEMME,
MALKE, } *Workingwomen in Goldin's factory.*

TSIPPE,
DOBBE, } *Women living with Isaac's family.*

HINDE,
SOZYE, } *Dobbe's daughters.*

GELYE, *Tsippe's daughter.*

VICHNE, *A shopkeeper*

The action takes place in a large city of the Jewish pale, Russia, in the early nineties of the nineteenth century.

ACT I

ISAAC SHEFTEL'S *cellar-home. Against the right-hand wall, two wooden beds, covered with rags. The sheets over the pillows are fairly black with dirt, and are stained here and there with yellow spots, the evidence of little children. In the center of the room a small four-legged table, without a tablecloth. Three chairs are placed about the table. The red paint, which once bedecked the table and the chairs, has faded to a dirty gray, with here and there a red spot visible. The chair to the left lacks a back. Against the left wall, in the foreground, stands a small chiffonier, on which are placed a small looking glass, three brass candlesticks, and a hat that was once black, but has become brown with age. Further back from the chiffonier, a chair, placed nearer to the center of the room. Nearby, the door to* TSIPPE'S *room. Next to the door, in the background, the large oven, with its opening facing the right wall. Between the oven and the left wall there is a bed of boards. Here is discovered* PINYE. *In the middle background is the door which leads to the outer rooms and to* DOBBE'S *room. When this opens there is visible the door to the street. Between the oven and the door to the outer rooms is a long, narrow kitchen bench. Under the bench a bucket. On the bench a few pots. Above* it, *some shelves, which contain a copper pan, a kneading board, and more pots. Aside of the bench, next to the oven, stand fire-forks, a baker's shovel, a broom. To the right of the door, a yellow cupboard, somewhat brighter at the top, for the bottom is covered with dust and dirt. A small piece of glass in the upper door of the cupboard is the only remnant of the panes which were once part of it. The hole is now stuffed from the inside with a large piece of blue paper, whose color is somewhat faded. Over the bed nearest the cupboard hang some clothes, covered with a sheet that is gray with dirt and threadbare in many places. At the side of this bed stands a cradle.— In the cellar there reigns semi-darkness, as in all cellar rooms whose windows are situated below the sidewalk. The windows are dark with dirt. Only from the bright light that becomes greenish after it has filtered through the dirty window panes, can one recognize that outside the life-giving sun is shining. The walls, once whitewashed, are black with soot, and discolored from mold and dampness. Here and there looks out a bright spot, like the sad eye of a one-eyed person, and makes the impression all the more melancholy by contrast. The ceiling is likewise black and sooty, and its plaster is crumbling. As to the floor, it is difficult to recognize what it is made of, whether of boards, stone, or Mother Earth itself. The dominant note is not so much one of poverty — which could be covered over — as of slovenliness, negligence, weary despair and hopeless debasement.*

Isaac Sheftel *is seated at the table, whittling a piece of wood. He is a young man, of about thirty, of*

spare build, hollow cheeks and blond beard. He
presses his pale, thin lips tightly together, often
biting the upper or lower one, including his short
mustache as he does so. His eyes are sunk deep beneath thick, shaggy eyebrows. His gaze is thought-
ful, keen, penetrating, and burns with an inner fire.
He wears a coat that is torn in the sleeves and at the
tails; it is buttoned only at the bottom, the other but-
tons being lacking. His shirt, visible because his
coat is unbuttoned at the top, and through the
holes in his sleeves, is unclean, and open, revealing
a hairy, sunken chest. His gray trousers are
patched at the knee with cloth of a much brighter
color. The patches look for all the world like windows. At the bottom the trousers are worn and
ragged. His shoes are a brownish yellow, with
twisted heels and torn soles. His head, uncovered,
is a mass of uncombed, thick, dark brown hair.—
Upon the table before him is an assortment of
wheels, smoothly whittled pieces of wood, a long,
wide leg of a machine, through which has been thrust
a long, round stick with holes on one side and a
wheel on the other. Between the wheel and the
stick, an axle, also perforated. There are on the
table also a compass, a handsaw, a gimlet, bits of
glass, thread, etc.

BAYLYE *is seated upon the forward bed, holding in her
arms* ELINKE, *a child of a year and a half, whom she
is nursing.* BAYLYE *is about* ISAAC'S *age; thin, flat-
chested, unclean, with rings of unwashed dirt about
her eyes. Her cheap calico dress and coat are in
tatters, and covered with patches. On her head a
cloth of undiscoverable color. It lies crooked, and*

from underneath falls over her forehead a shock of chestnut-colored hair. Her shoes have been unpolished for many days. The child at her breast is wearing a long shirt, much too large, which has been passed on to him by an older child.

PINYE is seated upon the board bed, and stares vacantly into the distance with an insane look. The blackish gray beard around his pallid face is thin; the hair of both his beard and his head is falling out. On his head, an old, greasy, torn hat. A cotton jacket, whose lining is almost all gone, covers his bare body. Over the jacket a worn out coat. When his coat opens, there are visible the thick fringes of the four-fringed scarf worn by all pious Jews, and a part of his drawers. Near the rear bed sits GISHINKE, a little girl of four, playing with her doll, which is made of a stick wound about by a rag. She is uncombed, and, like all the other cellar dwellers, unclean. She is little more than skin and bones, in tatters and barefoot. She is talking to her doll: "I'll dress you. . . . Don't cry. . . . I'll hit you, if you do! . . . Give you eat pretty soon. . . ."

Near the oven, DOBBE, a short, shriveled-up woman of fifty-five, her shaven head covered by a cloth wig. She is busy placing her pots in the oven.

It is about noon. The room is quiet, except for ISAAC's heavy cutting with the knife, GISHINKE's muttering to her doll, and the scraping of DOBBE's pots inside the oven, as she moves them about with the fire-fork. From TSIPPE's room, at intervals, comes the rhythmic noise of a stocking machine.

Isaac *stops whittling, inspects the piece of wood upon which he has been working, then the wheels that lie on the table before him. He frowns and bites his upper lip.*

Baylye *looks at him inquiringly.— For a time the stocking machine is silent*

Pinye [*rises slowly, wraps his cloak about him, stops at* Tsippe's *door and fixes his gaze upon it. Then he walks over to the table, looks at* Isaac's *work, walks back, observes* Gishinke *for a while, returns to the oven and stands motionless, his gaze lowered to his bed of boards. Gradually he raises his eyes, stares into the distance, and in a sepulchral voice, slowly turning about, he commences to drawl*]. All hea-ven is-s dead. Ear-earth is dead. God-d is d-dead. E-everything— [*Stops suddenly and lowers his head.*]

Dobbe [*puts the fire-fork back in its place, closes the oven and grumbles*]. It refuses to bake. A fine fire they must have made!

Baylye [*with an indignant motion of her head*]. It's never hot enough for her!

Dobbe [*as she goes out*]. And nobody can get dinner ready here until supper-time!

Baylye [*casting an angry look at* Dobbe *as she leaves, spits out scornfully*]. The old witch!

Pinye [*turning about*]. D-dead! D-dead! D-dead! E-everything. D-dead! Ev —

Baylye [*angrily*]. Stop your turning, will you! My head and my heart and all my insides are turning enough as it is.

Pinye [*stops short with a gaping mouth, his back to* Baylye. *He turns his head to the left, in* Baylye's *di-*

rection, and listens to her words. When she has finished, he turns his head back, lowers his gaze to the floor, and goes slowly to his place near the oven. He sits down as before].

SILENCE

Isaac [*deeply absorbed in his work, to himself*]. Right here is where I strike my difficulty. . . . Now, if I could manage to put, right here. . . .

Baylye [*venomously*]. How many times have I got to listen to that! "Right here . . . right here. . . ." And there's no end to it in sight!

Isaac [*wrinkles his forehead, his right hand at his work, his left fist clenched against his brow, as if in deep thought*].

Baylye. A fine thing! Takes a vacation for himself and doesn't go to work in the factory already the third day! Wants to invent machines! Such big profits we get from his inventions! Makes Goldin rich, that's all!

Isaac [*eyes Baylye from under his left hand, as if he would like to know what on earth she is talking about*].

Baylye. A fine matter! Three days' loafing! And God knows if he's through yet!

Isaac. If you'll keep gabbing like that all the time, I'll certainly never get through.

Baylye. I know. I'm only a nuisance. I . . .

Isaac [*hastily resumes work*].

Baylye [*casts a look of intense hatred at him, then turns her head to the wall. Elinke stops sucking at his mother's breast. Baylye covers her bosom and lowers the infant to her lap*].

Pinye [*as soon as it is quiet, he begins to drawl again*]. D-dead! D-dead! Empty. . . . No more. . . .

BAYLYE. Sit there and shut up, I tell you! Not a word!

PINYE [*stops short, mouth agape, slowly closing it*].

SILENCE

ISAAC [*works with nervous haste*].

BAYLYE [*watching him, bitterly, from the corner of her eye*].

GISHINKE [*from her place near the cupboard*]. Ma! What's here in the saucer? I want to eat it.

BAYLYE [*angrily, and in fright*]. Put that saucer right back where you found it! How many times have I told you not to touch that saucer under the closet! It has rat-poison in it!

GISHINKE. Rat-poison, is it? I want a little. Just a wee little piece.

BAYLYE [*jumps to her feet, holding* ELINKE *in her left arm, and runs over to* GISHINKE]. Put that saucer right back, I tell you! [*Tears a piece of the poison out of* GISHINKE's *hand, throws it back into the plate, thrusts the saucer under the closet with her foot, and spanks* GISHINKE *over the hands.*]

GISHINKE. Ow! Ow!

BAYLYE [*pushing her away from the closet*]. That's poison. People die from it. I'll kill you if you ever touch that saucer again. Sit down on the bed and be quiet or else go out into the street. [*Goes back to her place.*] She noses about everywhere. She'll poison herself before you know it.

TSIPPE [*enters from the door which leads outside. She is a woman of some fifty years. She carries two baskets, filled with apples and pears. She passes to her room. She wears a smooth wig, which lies crooked upon* her head; a calico dress and jacket, with a belt from which hangs a leather pocket].

GISHINKE [*busy with her doll*]. I'll go into the street.

BAYLYE. To the devil, for all I care. [*GISHINKE takes her doll and goes out.*] Don't run around too much, or get into a scrap, or I'll whip the skin off your back! [*Her gaze turns from GISHINKE to the cupboard, she kneels down to the floor and shoves the saucer further under the closet.*] It's I who ought to swallow the poison. And put an end to my wretched existence. [*She sits down again in her place.*]

TSIPPE [*enters from her room. She has put away her baskets, but the leather pocket still hangs from her belt; she goes to the oven, takes out a pot, looks into it and adds a little water*]. Hm! It's still raw! There you are! [*Puts the pot back into the oven and returns to her room.*]

BAYLYE. There's another hot-head for you! [*She puts ELINKE into bed and goes to the oven. The child begins to cry.*] Have a look here, will you, Isaac? Just have a look! That old hag went out and changed the pots all around until ours is 'way in the corner and hers is right over the hottest part. Just take a look, will you, Isaac? She'll drop dead before I'll let her get away with that! [*Busies herself with the oven.*]

ISAAC [*pondering over his work*]. It's bad. Nothing will come of it all.

BAYLYE [*putting back the fire-fork*]. Now! Her dinner can get ready with her pot over there, too. [*Returns to her place with an air of satisfaction and takes the infant into her arms again. With a voice full of hatred.*] And you, bawling all the time! I can't put him off my arms for a minute. [*Sits down and seats the* child in her lap, angrily. *The child falls asleep at once.*]

ISAAC [*leaves his work to pace about the room. He bites his lips, pressing them against his teeth with the index finger of his right hand. His left hand he passes across his forehead and through his hair*].

BAYLYE [*watches him, ironically*]. " Right here . . . right here." Ha-ha! — It'll be a matter of ten months, like with your press. Hm. . . . That's if anything at all comes out of all this fussing. . . . " Right here . . . right here. . . ." A fine state of things. Goes and gives himself a vacation!

ISAAC [*suddenly stopping*]. Perhaps you'll stop talking some time? [*Continues pacing about.*]

BAYLYE. You'll stuff my mouth, I suppose, so that I can't even say a word, eh? Well, then — go ahead. Stuff it! Here it is, stuff it! [*Mocking him.*] " Perhaps you'll stop talking some time!" I'm a fool that I should merely talk! I ought to take all these contraptions of yours and smash them to splinters. That would spare me all my talk, once and for all!

ISAAC [*grits his teeth, furrows his forehead and continues his nervous walking to and fro*].

BAYLYE. Why, anybody I'd tell this to would call me crazy to put up with it! Did you ever see? Takes a holiday for himself and stays out from work for three days! If there were only some chance of making a profit from it all, it wouldn't be so bad. Not on your life, though! He worked on that press of his for ten months, night after night — and what did he get out of it? A measly twenty roubles, and made Goldin rich! And what did you get from that braiding-machine? Wasted gallons of kerosene — that's all.

Isaac [*goes over to the table, takes hold of the wheel and leans his knee against the chair*].

Baylye [*somewhat more calmly*]. If you see that you can't make it work, throw it to the devil, and an end to the story. And you go back to work. Not kill three days —

Isaac [*begins to pace about as before*].

SILENCE

Notte Goldin [*enters from the street. He is past middle age, wears ear-locks, a wide beard, and thick, closely-cropped mustache. On his head a velvet hat. His trousers, boots and dark jacket are stained with greasy spots. The jacket is buttoned at the top and over it is a long, unbuttoned black coat, with long, wide pockets; a white wing collar. On his collar is the black ribbon from which hangs his watch. The watch is also attached to a heavy, silver chain, which is visible through the open coat. He keeps his hands in his pockets most of the time and as he speaks, calmly or excitedly, he drags and pulls and thrusts his coat-tails about. His face bears an excited expression, his speech is angry, and only rarely does he look straight into the face of the person he is addressing*].

Isaac [*when he notices* Goldin *he shudders nervously*].

Baylye [*looks triumphantly at* Isaac *as if to say, " I told you so! "*].

Goldin. Well, well. You're having a nice promenade, I see.

Baylye [*ironically*]. That's his way of thinking out his deep problems.

Goldin [*to* Isaac]. And you've been thinking in this manner for the past three days?

BAYLYE. There on the table you can see the result of all his marvelous brainwork. [*She picks up the wheels and the sticks and drops them one by one back upon the table.*]

GOLDIN [*goes over to the table and surveys the work*].

ISAAC [*walks over to the table, looks at* GOLDIN's *hand with the same absorbed thought as before, but with an expression of vexation at* GOLDIN's *interference*].

GOLDIN. And what do you call this?

ISAAC. A machine.

GOLDIN. A machine! Indeed! I can see for myself that it isn't a kneading board. What kind of machine?

BAYLYE. May he know as much about his brains, as he himself can tell of the machine. He stands there, puttering and puttering about and . . .

GOLDIN. Surely you must know what you're making. What sort of a contrivance is it? A tassel-machine?

ISAAC. So you know, then.

GOLDIN. Does it cost you money to talk?

ISAAC [*takes the work out of* GOLDIN's *hands and begins to put certain things together*].

GOLDIN [*looks on inquiringly*].

BAYLYE. That's just how he's been sitting there the whole three days, and it's all you can do to get a word out of him. Early Sunday morning he jumped out of bed; a precious idea had come to him! He didn't wash himself, and even forgot to say his prayers. He went straight to work. He's just as crazy as his old father. When he takes a notion into his head . . .

GOLDIN. But . . . he always used to carry on his experiments at night — how did it enter his head to do it by day, and not to come to work?

BAYLYE. May I know as much of his life, as I know of that! Day and night alike for the past three days, he sits there, poking away, whittling and contriving, contriving and whittling. You can't tear him away from the spot. There'd be half an excuse if he only had any profit from it all. But we know already the great fortunes he made on his first two inventions.

GOLDIN. Well, I didn't ask him to make them. It's better for me if he's at his bench, working. I'm piled up with orders now, and here his bench must be empty. He doesn't want to work? All right then, settled. So I know, and I get a man in his place. And that reminds me. I came here expressly to tell you that unless you come back to work this very forenoon, I'll give your job to another fellow. I can't lose any time waiting. My customers don't wait for me either.

BAYLYE. There! I knew his machines would bring us to this!

GOLDIN [*surveys the work in* ISAAC's *hand*]. Well, what'll it be? Really a machine for tassels? [*With impudent curiosity he takes the work from* ISAAC's *hand.*] Let's see what you're making, anyway.

ISAAC [*with repressed agony*]. You can't understand anything about it. You'll see when it's all finished.

GOLDIN. Then you really expect to finish it sometime?

BAYLYE. Sure. . . . When the Messiah comes. It'll be a long drawn out affair like the press . . .

GOLDIN. Well, you've heard what I said. For my part, let it take as long as two presses. It's no worry of mine.

BAYLYE. I know it's not your worry. Why should it be? The machine will sooner or later belong to you, anyway.

GOLDIN [*turns toward* PINYE, *hears* BAYLYE's *words, and makes a gesture as if to answer her; then he puts his right hand in his pocket, smacks his lips, and rolls his eyes, as if to say, "Bah! What's the use of talking to a woman?" Then he asks]:* Well, how are things with you, Pinye?

PINYE [*looks at* GOLDIN, *and commences to speak slowly*]. All heaven is dead. Earth is dead. God is dead . . .

GOLDIN. Hush! Hush! Pah! What kind of words are these?

BAYLYE. For us, God really has died.

GOLDIN [*excited*]. Wha — Wha — What kind of words are these? How can a person talk that way?

BAYLYE. What of it? It makes no difference.

GOLDIN. Tfu! Upon my word! How-how-how . . . Oh, well! You see. . . . That's why God punishes you. . . .

BAYLYE [*wipes her eyes with the corner of her jacket*]. This way or that way, it's all one. Our life is done for, anyway.

GOLDIN [*shaking his head and shrugging his shoulders*]. Well! [*Goes to the door.*] I warn you once more, I'll not wait much longer. If you don't come back to your work this forenoon, I'll put another man in your place. . . . I . . . I . . . I . . . Well! [*Kisses the mazuzah* * *and goes out.*]

SILENCE

BAYLYE. That's what it'll come to. He'll give your job to another man and we'll be left without a piece of bread.

---

* A little tin-box containing selections from the Scriptures written upon a piece of parchment. It is nailed on the door-post in the houses of all orthodox Jews.

Isaac. That's it! Keep on complaining! He won't give my place to anybody else.

Baylye [*sarcastically*]. Of course he won't! He can't run the factory without you! He needs you badly! How can he possibly do without you?

Isaac [*raising his gaze to her, suffering, but firm*]. All right then. So he *will* put another fellow in my place. And now stop plaguing me. I'll soon be through. Be quiet for a moment, at least.

Baylye [*wiping her eyes and talking to herself*]. A man goes and withdraws himself from the rest of the world and it doesn't bother him a hair's worth.

SILENCE

Pinye [*begins to walk slowly about the room, stopping a few times. He looks now at the floor, now into the distance, now about him, and then walks on. At length he comes to a stop near the chiffonier, looks it over for a while and turns his back to the oven. He directs his gaze again to the floor and drawls*]. Dead. Heaven. Earth. The whole world —

Baylye [*weeping to herself*]. If it were only true — and an end to our misery.

Pinye [*continuing*]. And God.

Baylye [*makes a gesture of despair*].

Pinye. Everything is dead.

Baylye. It's worse with me than with a dead person.

Pinye. Everything. Dead.

Baylye. Nobody must bear in hell what I endure here.

Pinye. Dead. Dead.

Baylye. If only the Almighty would take me to Him, then I'd really know that there is a God on earth.

PINYE. Dead. E-e-everything.

BAYLYE. Then I should feel as if I were delivered. . . .

ISAAC [*pale, agitated, breathing hard, groaning*]. Oh! Be quiet for a moment at least. Be quiet! [*Places both hands despairingly upon the edge of the table; his eyes express the deepest agony — soon he presses his forehead with both hands, leaning with his elbows on the table.*]

PINYE [*raises his head, cocks his left ear in* ISAAC's *direction and listens to his outcries with curiosity. Then he lowers his head as if pondering over something, and returns slowly to his place*].

SILENCE

BAYLYE [*dries her eyes*].

[*From the next room comes the groaning and moaning of the stocking-machine.*]

VICHNE [*enters. She is a woman of about fifty, in a bright calico jacket, from under which is visible another one of darker color. She wears a wide apron, and is covered with stains from flour, kerosene and oil. On her head, a smooth black wig from beneath which here and there falls some of her own hair, already gray. Over her large mouth plays a sweet smile, and her eyes dart about in every direction. She holds her left hand in a leather pocket which hangs under her apron, and she shakes her coins*]. Good morning to you!

BAYLYE [*gloomily*]. Good year to you, Vichnetshka.

VICHNE. I was in to see Dobbe. So I said to myself, "Well, as long as I'm already here, I must step in to have a look at Baylye." What's the news?

BAYLYE. News. Ah!

VICHNE [*sits down on the chair to the left of the table*]. And how goes it with his work?

BAYLYE. May I know as little about him as I know about that.

VICHNE [*taking one of* ISAAC's *hands down from his forehead*]. I say, Mr. Sheftel, won't you even look at me? Don't you look upon women?

ISAAC [*makes an unsuccessful attempt to smile. He tries to free his hand*].

VICHNE [*looks at him closely and releases his hand*].

ISAAC [*arises and paces about the room*].

VICHNE [*changes seats, taking the one* ISAAC *has just left. Then in a subdued voice to* BAYLYE]. Why is he so downcast?

BAYLYE. Yes, why is he? The lunatic!

VICHNE. To tell the truth, he does seem a bit deranged.

BAYLYE. He's plain crazy, just like his father. When he takes anything into his head he gets so wild over it, so bewildered, that he doesn't know whether he's in this world or the next. When he's in such a state neither fire nor earthquake can make any impression on him.

VICHNE [*observing* ISAAC *as he paces about*]. You'll wear out your shoes, Isaac.

BAYLYE. A lot he cares.

ISAAC [*engrossed in thought*]. The shoes aren't worth anything anyway.

VICHNE. Even if you're thinking out a new invention, you've got to be a man just the same. [*To* BAYLYE.] Banker Maggidson's son is an inventor, too. He's an engineer — studied at Moscow, and all his professors said that he was simply a wonder! — Ah! He's got a terribly smart head on his shoulders. And the machines that he invents, they say, are . . . why, enough to drive a person mad. And he's strong and stout — and I only

wish all my good friends had such red cheeks. I tell
you — all milk and blood! And his inventions are a
little better than Isaac's, I'll wager! He gets tens of
thousands of roubles for them. . . .

BAYLYE. Where's the wonder, where? The fellow
had a college education.

VICHNE. No, I mention all this to show that some people can think up machines without getting bewildered
and upset, and can be persons just like any other.

BAYLYE [*sarcastically*]. You hit upon the right one to
talk to. [*Nodding toward* ISAAC.] Do you call him a
man, too?

VICHNE [*surveying the work on the table*]. Is there
at least a good piece of money in it for him?

BAYLYE. A good piece, indeed! A fine piece of money
he'll get! He'll carry it to Goldin, and take whatever
he's offered.

VICHNE [*to* ISAAC]. If that's the case, Isaac, begging
your pardon, you're really not much of a man at that.

ISAAC [*paces about without saying a word*].

VICHNE [*to* BAYLYE]. Not much of a man at all.
How can a person be like that? If Goldin offers a low
price, let him take his machine to Bashkevitz or Levine.

BAYLYE. There! That's exactly what we've all been
telling him. "Take it in to Bashkevitz or Levine," we
urged. "Why must you give it to Goldin?" But he —
no use. He must have his machines near him. He
works in Goldin's place, so his machines must be there,
too. He can't part with them.

ISAAC [*stops. Places his right hand on his forehead.
Then he hurries over to the table, shoves all the wheels
and sticks to the left, sits down and resumes work.—*
VICHNE *and* BAYLYE *follow him with their eyes*].

VICHNE. That's the way. Brace up. Be a man. Sit down to your work, finish it, and see to it that you get a proper price for it. What do you care where the machine goes? The money'll come in handy, you may be sure. Then you can pay me the bill that you owe.— Do you know that it amounts to six roubles already?

BAYLYE [*frightened*]. Six roubles?

VICHNE. Yes, yes. Six roubles. What did you think? A week ago Monday, do you remember, it was four roubles and seventeen kopecks. Do you remember?

BAYLYE. And already six roubles, now!

VICHNE. What do you think? And I wanted to say, too, that it's time I saw a couple of roubles. And pretty soon, too. Because it'll soon be seven roubles and eight. . . . Vichne is a good woman, of course, but even Vichne will soon lose patience. I haven't yet robbed a bank. [*To* ISAAC.] Now if I were an inventor of machines, I might invent a money-machine, but as it is . . .

BAYLYE [*observes* ISAAC, *who is working away intently, apparently oblivious to the conversation*]. You see for yourself. There he sits, and doesn't even know we're here talking.

VICHNE. He hears, you may be sure. [*Slaps* ISAAC *on the shoulder.*] That's the idea. Work away, make a first-class machine, get a pile of money for it and settle your account with me. [*Arising.*] Well, I'll have to be going now. I've been away from the store for quite a while. I step in for a few moments here, another little while there, and that's how the time flies. Well, a good day to you!

BAYLYE. A good year to you, Vichnetshka!

VICHNE [*shaking* ISAAC]. A good day to you, Isaac.

Answer a lady, can't you, when she bids you good day!
Isaac. A good day to you, Vichne, a good day.
Vichne. Well, good day. [*Exit.*]

SILENCE

Baylye [*drying her eyes*]. Six roubles already.— She'll soon stop giving us on trust. It's mighty kind of her that she's let the bill run up as high as it is.— [*Ready to weep.*] And now you may lose your job, too. [*Bursts into tears.*]

SILENCE

Isaac [*works away nervously*].
Baylye [*gradually calms down*].
Gishinke [*comes running in from the street*]. Ma! I want to eat. [Baylye *dries her eyes.* Gishinke *pulls her by the skirt.*] I want to eat. Give me something to eat.
Baylye [*thrusting her away*]. Away from me!
Gishinke [*frightened*]. I want to eat.
Baylye. All right. Under the closet there's the saucer of poison. Take it, eat it, and let me be rid of you once and for all.
Gishinke. I don't want poison. I want to eat. Poison is for rats. Give me something. I want a piece of bread. [*Pulls* Baylye's *skirt again.*]
Baylye. Away from me, do you hear! [*Thrusts her away.* Gishinke *falls, and bursts into loud crying.*]
Isaac [*ceases working. He is pale, agitated, and casts an angry look at* Baylye. *He arises, goes to the cupboard, takes out bread, cuts off a slice and gives it to* Gishinke]. Here, Gishinke, and don't you cry. We'll soon have dinner. Get up, like a good little girl, and

don't you cry. [*He lifts her up and goes back to his place. For a time he buries his face in both his hands. Then he resumes his work.*]

GISHINKE [*in one hand the slice of bread, her other hand on her head, goes over to* ISAAC, *leans against his knee, and between her sobs eats the bread*].

BAYLYE [*dries her eyes, her head turned to the wall*]. She'll cry worse than that yet, when there'll be nothing at all left to eat. Oh, what a life, what a life! [*Breaks out into lamentation.*]

ISAAC [*at first he applies himself nervously to his work, then he drops it with a loud bang, leaning back against the chair, looking vacantly before him into the distance, tired, exhausted, his hands thrust into his trousers pockets*].

BAYLYE [*restrains her weeping and dries her eyes*].

GISHINKE [*has ceased crying, and is now quietly eating her bread*].

SILENCE

GISHINKE. Shall we soon have dinner? [ISAAC *is silent.*] Pa, shall we soon have dinner?

ISAAC [*straightens up*]. Yes, Gishinke, yes. [*Begins to work once more.*]

SILENCE

GISHINKE. Pa, are you making a machine? — Are you making a good machine? — Will the wheels turn? — Will you show it to me? [*Takes hold of the long stick with the holes in it.*] What's this, pa?

ISAAC. Let it stay there. Don't touch anything.

GISHINKE. Is this a machine, too? [*Eats her bread.*]

SILENCE

GISHINKE. And shall we soon have dinner?

ISAAC. Yes, Gishinke, yes. And do keep still.

BAYLYE [*angrily*]. Go away from him! What are you bothering him for?

GISHINKE [*stands for a moment sullenly, and then goes away from* ISAAC. *She picks up her rag-doll, sits down on the floor near her father, and talks to her doll*]. We'll soon have dinner. . . . I'll give you some, too. . . . But you must be quiet. . . . [*Soon she arises and goes out.*]

SILENCE

TSIPPE [*appears at her door, stops, and speaks to some one in her room*]. It must be ready by now. I can't wait any longer. [*Goes to the oven, opens it, and is about to thrust in a fire-fork.*] What's this! Who's been here now? [*Casts a venomous glance in* BAYLYE'S *direction.*] What do you say to that! I tell you, it's — [*Busying herself about the oven.*] May the hands of the one who did this be paralyzed, Lord of the Universe! That's a gall that it would be hard to meet anywhere! To go and purposely shove my pot 'way out in front. How am I going to have it ready? I've got to be going right away and here the meat hasn't even begun to cook. [*Puts down the fire-fork.*] I'd just like to know whose work that was!

BAYLYE [*with heat*]. And what do you mean by shoving all the pots aside and putting yours right in the hottest part of the oven? Do you think that the next person's meat mustn't be cooked just as well as your own? Aren't we supposed to have dinner, too?

TSIPPE [*with piercing irony, shaking her head*]. Ah, Baylinke, Baylinke! One must have the heart of a robber. . . .

GELYE [*appears at* TSIPPE's *door. She is a young lady of some twenty-five years, in an unbuttoned white blouse. An unfinished stocking in her hand*]. What's up? More trouble?

TSIPPE. Do you imagine the dinner's ready yet? Not a bit of it! It hasn't even started to cook. And where do you think our pot was standing all this time? Just come here, and take a look. I open up the oven — and there I find my pot 'way in front. . . .

BAYLYE [*arises and places* ELINKE *in the cradle.* ELINKE *commences to cry;* BAYLYE *rocks him*]. And that's where I'll always put it. Other people are persons, too, and they need to eat as well as you.

DOBBE [*enters*]. What kind of a pot fight do you call this?

TSIPPE. Why, just listen. Here I must be going right away,— and I come to the oven, you understand, and I see my pot standing —

BAYLYE [*runs over to* DOBBE]. She goes and shoves all the other pots aside, and puts her own in the best place. . . . [*Runs back to the cradle and continues to rock.*]

DOBBE [*goes to the oven and opens it*]. Look at this, will you! My pot's right near the oven-door! I suppose mine doesn't need to cook at all!

BAYLYE [*pointing to* TSIPPE]. Ask her. She was just now at the oven.

TSIPPE [*with heat*]. I didn't touch your pot. May I live so . . .

BAYLYE [*leaving the cradle. To* DOBBE]. You should have seen. She shoved all the pots aside. . . . [*Goes back to the cradle.*]

GELYE. And suppose she did put her pot right over the burning coals? What then? She must go away, and you're always at home. You don't have to bring Isaac dinner to-day. [*Ironically.*] He's at home too busy with his machines.

BAYLYE [*returning excitedly near to the cradle, pushing back her hair, and tying her head covering better about her neck*]. Other people are persons too. They need to eat as well as you! [*To* GELYE.] And his machines are none of your business, I'll have you understand.

DOBBE [*busy with her pot*]. All I know is that my pot hasn't even begun to cook.

GELYE [*sarcastically*]. Just see how indignant she became because somebody said a word about her husband's machines.

BAYLYE. You've got no business talking about my husband's machines.

GELYE. Really! Well! Well! [*From the rear door there enter* HINDE *and* SOZYE *with sewing in their hands.* HINDE *is a girl of twenty-one,* SOZYE *is seventeen.* HINDE *is attractively combed. Her black waist, with white polka-dots, and her skirt, are already quite worn out, but they become her very well. The high collar of her waist is tight about her neck and is buttoned over her left shoulder.* SOZYE *imitates her elder sister in everything, and is a trifle " fresh."*]

HINDE. Hush! What kind of a wedding do you call this?

BAYLYE [*still busy with her hair*]. She, too, has to talk about his machines!

DOBBE [*to her daughters*]. Any one would think we don't pay rent here. We aren't allowed to put our pots into the oven.

BAYLYE [*pointing to* TSIPPE]. It's all her doings. All hers. She shoved all the pots aside and . . .

Tsippe. May your hands wither . . .

Orke Goldin [*appears at the rear door. A young man of twenty-five or twenty-six. Dressed like a dandy, beard shaven, curled mustache. He wears a large overcoat, bright colored shoes, his yellow derby on a slant, a stiff collar, with a loud tie in which sticks a diamond pin. Rings on the fingers of both hands. He carries a heavy cane, with a staghorn top. He stops on the threshold and calls out*]. Ahu! Ahu! What kind of a fair do you call this? [*The cries of the women subside.* Gelye *disappears into her room,* Tsippe *takes out her pot and follows* Gelye. Dobbe *pushes her daughters toward the door, but they pretend to be occupied with their needlework, and remain in the room.* Baylye *takes from the cradle* Elinke, *who has by this time reached his highest notes; she places him on her left arm and spanks him, then takes him in her hands and rocks him there, as she goes about the room.*]

Orke [*stepping into the room. Merrily*]. Why! You're having a jolly time here!

Baylye. May my enemies enjoy such jolly times! When God wants to punish a person, He certainly gives good measure. . . . As if bad neighbors weren't enough, here comes . . .

Orke [*who has meanwhile gone over to* Isaac]. And he sits and works away, and it doesn't bother him a bit. Well, my genius! How's your invention getting along?

Isaac [*with an effort*]. I don't know yet.

Baylye. The devil alone knows. And a lot more he knows, besides!

Sozye. If he didn't know, he wouldn't be working at it, would he?

Baylye. The lunatic!

Orke [*bends over the table*]. Let a fellow see what

you're making, there, won't you? Is that for tassels? [*Picks up a wheel.*] Where does this belong? [*Picks up another part and attaches it to the wheel.*] Does this go here? Well, Mr. Sphinx, say something. [HINDE *laughs and* SOZYE *follows suit.*] Are you reciting the Eighteen Benedictions now, that you have to stand so silent? [HINDE *and* SOZYE *laugh louder.*]

BAYLYE. Other people may talk and laugh as loudly as they please, and he doesn't object a bit. But just let *me* say a word, and he'll attack me like a mad dog.

ORKE [*takes a round piece of wood and squeezes it into a hole somewhere in the machine, which* ISAAC *is holding in his hand*].

ISAAC [*takes it out of* ORKE's *hand, lays it down on the table and continues his work*].

ORKE [*keeps nosing about* ISAAC's *work*].

BAYLYE. Nobody's ever in his way, except me.

DOBBE [*at the door, to her daughters*]. What are you standing there for? Haven't you a room of your own? Go into your own room and stay there.

HINDE. All right. All right. [*Turns to* BAYLYE *and shows her what she's working on.*] See the nice shirt I'm making. . . .

DOBBE [*disappears, grumbling*]. They won't budge. . . .

ORKE [*to* ISAAC]. No, no. Wait. . . . Put this over there. . . . No, you're making a bad job of it. Ah! I tell you, put this over there. . . . Never mind, take my advice. I tell you. . . . [*Holds* ISAAC *with his left hand, and with his right hand takes the machine.*]

ISAAC [*with restrained anger and intense suffering*]. Let me alone, won't you? You don't know what I want.

ORKE. You don't know yourself what you want. I know just what to do here.

ISAAC. Orke, please go away from me.

ORKE [*hitting* ISAAC's *head derisively*]. You're a dunce. You've got a wooden head. [*To the girls.*] As true as I am a Jew, I understand the contrivance better than he does. If he'd only let me, I'd finish the thing for him in a jiffy.

HINDE [*coquettishly*]. You merely think so.

ORKE [*impudently*]. Do you want me to show you an even better trick?

HINDE. Let's see.

ORKE. Too many people around.

HINDE and SOZYE [*blush. Their faces express embarrassment and indignation.* HINDE *turns to* BAYLYE *as if to say something to her*].

ORKE [*looks triumphantly at the girls, with an air of intense self-satisfaction. He notices* PINYE, *and turns to him, jocosely*]. Well, Reb Pinye, what is it that's dead?

PINYE [*raises his eyes to* ORKE *and lowers them immediately. He answers quickly*]. All Heaven's dead.

ORKE. And who else?

PINYE. The Earth is dead. God is dead. . . .

ORKE. And were you to His funeral?

PINYE. I was.

HINDE and SOZYE [*laugh*].

ORKE. Where did they bury Him?

PINYE. In the dead heaven.

ORKE. And they covered Him with earth?

BAYLYE [*to* ORKE]. Your father ought to be hearing this.

ORKE. My father would be the first one to put a contribution into the charity-box if God died.

BAYLYE. Indeed! [*To the girls.*] And what are you two giggling about? Is this proper talk to listen to? They even laugh at it!

HINDE [*laughs*]. I can't help laughing at the old man's answers.

BAYLYE [*angrily*]. And what is there to laugh at in a lunatic's talk?

DOBBE [*enters in a huff*]. They've planted themselves here and they refuse to budge. [*Goes to the oven.*]

BAYLYE. This young sport's trying to be smart, and they laugh at whatever he says.

DOBBE [*to her daughter, threateningly*]. What are you standing here for? I'll take the fire-fork and . . .

HINDE [*sharply*]. If you want to do something in the oven, why do it.

ORKE. Your mother beats you with the fire-fork, eh?

DOBBE [*taking her pot out from the oven*]. Come in, now, and eat. [*At the door.*] I'll pour your soup right away.

HINDE and SOZYE [*follow her with evident unwillingness*].

ORKE [*calling after them*]. Good appetite!

HINDE and SOZYE [*at the door. Laughing*]. Thank you. [*They disappear.*]

ORKE [*noses about* ISAAC's *work again*]. Well, how long is it going to take you to finish all this?

ISAAC [*shrugging his shoulders*].

ORKE. What are you shrugging your shoulders about? Eh? My father sent me to warn you, for the last time, that he'll put another man in your place. He's not fooling. He means what he says.

ISAAC [*shrugs his shoulders as before*].

BAYLYE. Shrugs his shoulders!

ORKE. There's nothing to shrug your shoulders about!

You come back to work to-day or to-morrow. Nobody needs your machines, I'll have you understand. And if they *will* need them, they'll be invented without your assistance. Better come back to work. [*To* BAYLYE.] See to it that he returns to work. We'll certainly put a man in his place.

BAYLYE. I've been after him for the past three days.

ORKE [*arises, about to go. Ironically*]. If he must tinker around with the "machine," let him work at it by night. Let him stay up all night for all I care.

TSIPPE [*appears at her door with both baskets. To* GELYE, *within*]. Then go, right away.

GELYE [*appears at the door. She is turned away from the audience and is buttoning her waist. She casts a glance at* ORKE]. All right. All right. Can't you see I'm dressing?

TSIPPE [*goes about the room, grumbling*]. Bah! What a meal that was! Everything raw!

ORKE [*sits down again. To* GELYE]. What did you run away for, Miss?

GELYE. I wanted to run away, so I did.

ORKE. I don't bite young ladies.

GELYE. I'm not afraid of being bitten. I've got teeth of my own. [*Disappears into her room.*]

ORKE [*nudges* ISAAC *with his elbow*]. Say, boy! You've got some sweet neighbors here! I'll have to be a more frequent visitor to your home.

BAYLYE. In that case they'll never want to leave our room.

ORKE [*curling his mustache*]. Am I really a good-looking chap?

BAYLYE. Much difference it makes to them. . . . A goose, a duck,— as long as it's a fowl. . . .

ORKE [*to* ISAAC]. Your wife isn't much at giving compliments.

BAYLYE [*cuttingly*]. I like to tell the truth.

GELYE [*enters from her room. She wears a yellow hat, a blue skirt and a bright tippet. Under her arm a small bundle. She walks to rear door*].

ORKE [*arises*]. Well, remember that you must return to work. If you're not there by to-morrow morning, you may be sure your job will go to another fellow, and you needn't trouble to come again. [*Hurries after* GELYE.]

BAYLYE [*stands motionless at the rear door, much surprised that both* GELYE *and* ORKE *are about to leave together*].

ORKE [*opens the door to the street, invites* GELYE]. If you please; ladies first. [HINDE *and* SOZYE *appear at their door.* ORKE *lifts his hat and bows.*] Good day!

HINDE and SOZYE [*laugh*]. Good day, gracious sir! [GELYE *and* ORKE *leave.*]

BAYLYE [*turns away from the door in anger and disgust. She spits out and swallows a curse.* HINDE *and* SOZYE *step into the room.* BAYLYE *does not deign to look upon them*].

HINDE. Is that old Goldin's son?

BAYLYE [*does not even reply nor look at* HINDE].

HINDE. Such a dude! Not a bit like his father!

BAYLYE. Fine men, both of them! Damn them!

HINDE. Beard shaved off, curly mustache. . . . [*Makes a gesture over her upper lip as if she were curling mustache.*] His derby cocked to one side. [*Makes a gesture as if placing her hat to one side.*]

SOZYE. A regular swell!

HINDE. Rings on his fingers. Did you see all the rings he wears?

BAYLYE [*angry and impatient*]. I've got other worries on my head besides counting the rings he wears.

HINDE [*as if* BAYLYE *had not addressed her*]. And the dainty pair of shoes. . . .

BAYLYE [*with an outcry*]. And that's all you've got to worry about, is it?

DOBBE [*at her door, to her daughters*]. What's that? Here again? Haven't you anything to do?

BAYLYE. They've started to talk about how Goldin's darling son was dressed. They've got nothing else to worry about.

DOBBE [*thrusting her daughters out*]. Out. Off to your work. Or else I'll take a fire-fork and . . .

BAYLYE. As soon as they see a pair of pants they go wild. [*Turns about and looks angrily at* ISAAC.]

SILENCE

ISAAC [*looks despairingly at the machine in his hands. Sighs*]. It doesn't work, no matter what I do.

BAYLYE [*stops suddenly between the table and the bed, and exclaims explosively*]. What do you say now? He won't put another man in your place, eh?

ISAAC [*in despair. Looks at his work with lifeless eyes*].

BAYLYE [*more sharply*]. I tell you, Isaac, my patience has its limits. . . .

ISAAC [*more despairingly than ever*]. It simply won't work, no matter what I do.

BAYLYE [*more heatedly*]. I tell you, I'll take your whole contraption and smash it to splinters. I'll dump it into the fire. . . . I'll . . .

ISAAC [*bitterly*]. H'm. [*Shakes his head despairingly.*]

BAYLYE. I'll show you that I've got a little say in the matter, too. I won't let you do whatever you please and leave us to starve of hunger. [*Her voice rises to a high pitch.*] Do you hear what I'm saying to you or not? I tell you, I'll . . .

ISAAC [*pale, trembling all over, his teeth clenched, he dashes all his work to the floor. He sinks down into the chair leaning heavily against its back, stretches out his feet, thrusts his hands into his pockets, and stares blankly at the edge of the table*].

BAYLYE [*her words freeze on her lips. She looks at* ISAAC *in fright*].

PINYE [*looks for a moment at the wheels and sticks that have rolled over to him, and bends slowly toward them*].

CURTAIN

ACT II

GOLDIN's *factory. A large wide room. To the left, two looms. Behind the second loom a high fire-place. In the right wall, two windows whose panes are of ground glass. Before the further of these windows is a third loom. Before the front window, a table with two chairs. Between the table and the loom stand* ISAAC's *press and machine. At the rear, a door, which leads to the yard on the right and the office on the left. Between the fire-place and the door a small table and a chair. In the middle of the room, front, a table with four chairs placed about it. To the right of the door, in the corner, there lean large hides, a couple of old scabbards, large rolls of cardboard. Across the rear wall extend shelves, on which are piled all sorts of cardboard, little chests, pieces of cloth of every color, and old epaulettes. The floor is littered with scraps of paper, cardboard, cloth, needles, gold threads, spangles, strips of galloon, etc. On the center table there are four cloth plates on which lie white, yellow and silver threads and spangles, and epaulettes, in various stages of completion. On the rear table, braid ready to be made into epaulettes.*

It is noon. Near the center table, his back to the door, sits ZELIG, *finishing his meal. He is about twenty-five; long, dark, uncombed hair; his beard is trimmed short; small mustache. He wears over his trousers a gray, hand-sewed shirt, tied around with a red ribbon with tufts. Before him are a plate, knife, spoon and fork. On the sill of the forward window, which is half open, sits* SENDER. *He is looking out into the yard, and whistling a tune. He is of* ZELIG's *age; his hair is chestnut-color, curly and parted in the middle; no beard, and thick, red curled mustache; wears a smock, collar and small tie, vest and coat. Between the two looms at the left, lies old* MICHEL. *He is almost gray, with a mixture of yellowish hair. Wears no coat. Over his shirt, which is open at the breast, is visible the four-fringed scarf worn by all orthodox Jewish men. At the rear table sits* YOSHKE, *a youngster of some fourteen or fifteen years, his head resting on his left hand, his right holding a pencil with which he plays on the table. His shoes are several sizes too large for him.— From the office comes the frequent ringing of a bell, which is attached to the door that leads in from the outside to the office.*

ZELIG [*his meal completed, he leans against the back of his chair, picks his teeth with a match, exhales his breath noisily, and turns to* YOSHKE *with the air of a distinguished guest*]. Waiter! A bottle of port! — Right away, now. I have no time. I say, waiter!

YOSHKE. At once, sir! [*From under the fireplace he takes an old kerosene bottle and brings it to him, leisurely, with a loud scraping of his large shoes.*] Here you are. Excuse the slight odor of kerosene.

ZELIG [*with an expression of dissatisfaction*]. My dear sir, what liberty is this you're taking? If you have no port, bring me some Bordeaux, or Chateau La-pfu-ique.

Yoshke [*scarcely moving, he drags out from under the fireplace an oil-stained beer-bottle, broken at the neck*]. This will delight you extremely, sir.

Zelig [*utters a confused cry, ending with*] You impertinent ass!

Michel [*waking from his nap*]. Ha! Zelig's at his jokes again!

Zelig [*puts the bottle back and, returning to his place, assumes the same position as before*].

SILENCE

Sender [*whistles as if he were signaling to somebody through the window*].

Zelig. The idea! Not to have my wine after my meal! Well, I don't come to this restaurant again! [*Thrusts his plate away from him.*] Waiter! The bill!

Michel. Devil take that clown! He doesn't let me sleep.

Zelig [*curls his mustache. His expression is as serious as ever*].

Sender [*calls to some one outside the window, in a subdued voice, at the same time making signs with his hand*]. Where were you, anyway? Just finished eating? You must have had seven courses!

Zelig [*jumping up*]. What? That stout one? [*Leaps over to the window where* Sender *is sitting. Looks out and begins to make all manner of bows.*] Good day! How goes it? [*To* Sender.] It seems to me she gains weight every day.

Sender [*to the girl in the opposite building*]. Weren't you over to Drovitz's dancing-school last night? No? Were you? Did you do much dancing?

Zelig [*to* Sender]. Ask her where Bashe is. [*In*

a subdued voice.] Where's Bashe? Ba-a-ashe! — That tall girl! In the next room? Tell her to come to the window. [*In the same breath, but much lower.*] Devil take you! — [*Louder.*] She's busy, you say? Busy, now?

SENDER. Just a second. I'll make a date with her for the park this evening. [*Loudly, through the window.*] Are you doing anything to-night?

ZELIG. Make it for Saturday in the woods.

SENDER [*through the window*]. Then let's meet in the park. In that long lane. The long one!

ZELIG [*helping him*]. In the lo-o-o-ong one — [*Under his breath.*] Ears as large as a donkey's, yet she can't hear. [*Aloud.*] Saturday, in the woods.

SENDER [*shouting*]. No, Saturday at Drovitz's.

ZELIG [*hitting him*]. To the deuce with you! The woods is a better place. [*Shouting through the window.*] The woods is better. Isn't it? No? You prefer Drovitz's? [*Pointing with his finger.*] Bashe coming along too? Yes? That's fine. Let's have a dance on it. [*Begins the "Blue Danube," blowing through his lips like a cornet, and dances. His arms are raised, swaying in the air, his body lowered and his knees bent. He dances thus for a while, until he has danced over to old* MICHEL *and falls on top of him.*]

MICHEL [*kicks him, pushing him away*].

ZELIG. Pardon me. Pardon me. . . . Hey there! Ow! Ow! No kicking, now! No kicking!

MICHEL. I'll split your head for you, you clown!

ZELIG [*arising, and dusting himself*]. What do you think of him? He kicks! [*Runs over to the window, where* SENDER *has been making signs to the girl across the way, and shouts across the yard*]. Ow! An old horse just kicked me!

MICHEL [*mumbling*]. Plague take him!

ZELIG [*to* SENDER]. And meanwhile you've already made a date with her. [*He, too, begins to make signs across the yard with his fingers, as if engaging in deaf-and-dumb language. From the yard comes a chorus of laughter and girlish voices. Soon there enter* BERRE, HILYE, LEIVIK, MALKE, *and* TEMME.]

ZELIG [*drops his deaf-and-dumb conversation and turns to those who have just come in. He addresses them in the voice of their employer,* GOLDIN]. What — what do you call this? Coming in so late! Once you people leave the place, you get lost altogether!

MICHEL [*straightening up*]. He doesn't close his mouth for a second.

BERRE [*a man of forty-five, long yellow beard, a large broad nose, red from drinking; a broad, knotty face. He wears a long black torn coat, that has turned green with age. He removes his hat, puts on an old, velvet skull-cap, which he takes out of his inside pocket, and gets busy near the loom at the right*].

HILYE [*somewhat over twenty. He needs a shave; his mustache is short and black; his black hair is cut quite close to his head. He wears a smock, and collar, but no tie. Sits down upon* YOSHKE's *table and begins to roll a cigarette*].

LEIVIK [*in the middle twenties, clean shaven, and neatly dressed in a grayish suit, smock, collar and necktie. Goes over to the window near* SENDER *and looks out into the yard*].

MALKE [*an elderly girl, coquettishly dressed in a tight-fitting bodice. She removes the plate from the table and puts it on a shelf*].

TEMME [*a young girl, with a dreamy expression. Stops before* ZELIG *with a broad smile*].

ZELIG [*still imitating the boss*]. They become new people from the moment they stop working. That crowd goes off and they forget to come back. And this lazy lout [*pointing to* MICHEL] lies down to snooze and you can't wake him up with a hammer. From this day forward, I forbid all going out for dinners, and all sleeping.

MALKE. Maybe you'll raise our wages, too, boss?

ZELIG. What! What! What else will you ask? Raise your wages! Indeed!

LEIVIK and SENDER [*return from the window with loud laughter*].

ZELIG [*very inquisitive. He forgets the rôle he has assumed*]. What was that? What were you people doing there? [*Runs over to the window, but sees nothing, so he turns back to* SENDER *and* LEIVIK, *who are still laughing.*] Did that cranky old forelady come to the window? — What's the joke? Out with it! [*Assuming* GOLDIN'S *voice and manner again.*] And you fellows could stand at the window all day, flirting with the girls! A fine bunch of workers I have! Not worth the dirt they step on!

LEIVIK [*stops laughing*]. You see, the old lady came by. So he . . .

MALKE and TEMME [*at the window*]. Isaac is coming! Isaac is coming! [*All the workers rush to the window.* MICHEL *gets up from the floor. There are cries of* "Welcome, Isaac!" . . . "Greetings!" "Have you got the machine with you?" . . .]

SENDER. I don't see him carrying any machines.

HILYE. He doesn't look any too cheerful. [*The workers turn to the door, expectantly.*]

ZELIG. Let's receive him with a loud hurrah and a march of triumph!

Isaac [*enters, pale, sad, dejected. He is greeted with a lusty "Hurrah!"*].

Zelig [*blows a march through his closed lips, waving his hands like a music-director*].

Yoshke and Temme [*hum the tune also*].

Isaac [*steps aside from the crowd, sadder and more dejected than ever, and walks over to the loom in the left foreground. He is plainly suppressing a bitter outburst*].

Berre. What's the trouble, Isaac? — Where's your new machine?

Isaac [*silent*].

Hilye. I guess it's all up with the machine.

Isaac [*throwing off his hat, angrily and bitterly*]. Shout "Hurrah!" Shout!

Leivik. Isn't the machine done yet?

Hilye. Isn't it done *yet*, or will it never be done?

Zelig. Or did your sweet better-half drive you out of the house?

Sender. Or are you pregnant with an idea for a brand new invention?

Isaac [*busying himself about the loom. Angrily*]. What are you pestering me for? What worry is it of yours?

Michel. Really, what worry of ours is it? Really. Really.

Zelig. Hush! You mustn't talk to our famous engineer. Hush! Quiet. . . . [*Walks on tiptoe, raising his feet high in the air. An alarm clock sounds the return to work. The men and women run to their places.* Zelig, Hilye, Malke, *and* Temme *go to the center table:* Zelig *at the left,* Malke *at the right,* Temme *at the back, and* Hilye *at the front;* Sender *and* Leivik *go to the table near the window:* Leivik *at the back,* Sender at the front; YOSHKE *goes to the table furthest back.* MICHEL *and* BERRE *remain near* ISAAC. *They, too, look dejected, and are silent.*]

ISAAC [*sits down to his work*].

MICHEL [*looks at him sadly*]. Did it all come to nothing? — Was it too hard to put together? — Will it take long? [*Seeing that he receives no reply, he sighs and casts his eyes to the floor, crestfallen.*]

BERRE [*sighs. Then both he and* MICHEL *proceed to their looms.* MICHEL *near* ISAAC, BERRE *to the loom at the right*].

ORKE [*appears at the door. Noticing* ISAAC, *he strikes an attitude, as if to say, " Ha! He is here! " He is about to step into the room, but suddenly recalls something and returns to the office*].

ZELIG [*with a mock sigh*]. Ah! The invention refused to be invented!

MALKE. And meanwhile he lost two and a half days of work.

HILYE. Well, let him not be so ambitious to become an inventor.

LEIVIK. That's easy to say. It's not a matter of mere wanting to be. It's a thing that's part of a person's very soul. I remember, when I was a youngster, I had a deep desire to become a painter. . . .

SENDER. You mean a sign-painter, perhaps?

LEIVIK. Every scrap of paper I'd pick up, I'd cover with pictures: People, soldiers, a horse . . .

HILYE. Yourself, in other words.

LEIVIK. At home and in the Hebrew school I used to be whipped without mercy, because all I did was draw pictures. And when they apprenticed me to a lacemaker, I cried my eyes out. . . .

SENDER [*with mock-tears*]. Boo-hoo!

LEIVIK. And to this very day, when I look at a good painting, I become so moody, and feel that there's something in me that is powerfully attracted to the picture.

ZELIG. Ah! In me, too!

HILYE. Ah!

LEIVIK. And at other times, when I sit thinking, I get such a powerful impulse to draw. . . .

ZELIG. And how I'd like to be an actor!

HILYE. A clown in the circus, maybe?

ZELIG. No, a real actor. And come out on the stage and declaim. . . . [*He places his left hand over his heart, raises his right hand high in the air, throws back his head and declaims.*] "How dear thou art, my precious heart!"

SENDER. Ah!

ZELIG [*continuing*]. "Thou angel . . ."

TEMME. I, too, would really like to go on the stage.

MALKE [*sarcastically*]. Well! What do you think of our new leading lady!

HILYE [*to* TEMME *and* ZELIG]. I'll tell you what! Why don't you two go on the stage in partnership and make — a troupe.

ZELIG [*suddenly falls to his knees before* TEMME].

TEMME [*frightened*]. Oh!

ZELIG [*stretching out his hand*]. Come to my arms, crown of my head. [*General laughter.*]

MICHEL and BERRE [*look upon the merriment with shaking of their heads. Footsteps are heard behind the office door*].

ZELIG [*jumps to his feet. The workers suddenly apply themselves very industriously to their work*].

MICHEL. There's a crowd for you!

BERRE. One is worse than the other.

MICHEL. Not worth the earth they step on.

Berre. Tramps . . . loafers . . .

Orke [*enters, and walks straight over to* Isaac]. Well, how goes it with your invention?

Zelig. It refused to be invented.

Orke. What? Nothing really came of it? Have you got it here?

Yoshke. The famous engineer is too busy to be disturbed now.

Berre. You shut up, you!

Zelig [*attempts to pull* Isaac's *chair from under him*].

Isaac [*furious*]. You clown, you. Keep your hands to yourself!

Orke. I told him right away, the moment I looked at the thing, that he was simply wasting his time at it. I saw at once that his effort was all misspent. And when I tried to give him a point or two . . .

Leivik. Who? You wanted to show him how to do it?

Orke. Upon my word, if he had only let me, I would have finished the thing for him in a jiffy.

Zelig [*crowing*]. Cock-a-doodle-doo!

Yoshke [*sneezes mockingly*]. Kerchoo!

Leivik [*to* Orke]. How long is it since you've become such a smarty?

Sender. You can't deny that he's an expert glutton.

Isaac [*turning to the men and women*]. Much he knows . . .

Hilye. That's it. Say something.

Orke [*sits down on the corner of the table near* Zelig]. But I tell you, he's got some swell-looking girls for neighbors! . . . [*He is at a loss for words to express his delight, and scratches his head with his right hand.*]

SENDER. There! Now you said something worth hearing!

MICHEL and BERRE [*cast significant glances at one another and sigh. The office bell rings.* ORKE *runs into the office*].

ZELIG [*calling after him*]. Drat that bell! Has to ring just when things are beginning to get interesting!

LEIVIK. My! What a connoisseur he's become all of a sudden!

MALKE. The simpleton! He can't add one and one!

BERRE. I'd enjoy giving a drubbing to a swell-head like that!

MICHEL. His old man is just the same. Knows it all.

MALKE. Only with his mouth.

LEIVIK. Did he really want to show you how to do it, Isaac?

MALKE. You can't talk to him to-day,— our silent inventor.

ZELIG. Not a word.

LEIVIK. I can imagine how he must have bothered him over there this morning.

BERRE. He's an awful bore, when he gets going.

HILYE. He doesn't bore me.

TEMME. I should say not.

HILYE. What are you blushing about?

TEMME. If you two get fresh with me once more, you'll hear from me.

ZELIG [*putting his arms around* TEMME's *waist*]. What? You dare to hurt my little Temme? [*Caresses her cheek.*] Tell me, dear little Temme, what did the naughty people do to you?

TEMME [*thrusting him away*]. Let me go, you clown. [*Enter* ORKE.]

MALKE [to ORKE]. Quick now. Tell us some more about those neighbors of Isaac's.

HILYE. What do you want, anyway? [To ORKE.] She, too!

ORKE [*lighting a cigarette, and puffing it so that it will get well started, goes over to the center table and sits down on its edge, near* ZELIG]. I tell you, boys, there's something to see there. He lives in a regular Garden of Eden. [To ISAAC.] What's the name of that girl I left with?

ZELIG. Quick work! He's been out with one of them already!

ORKE. I should say! But what's her name, Isaac? — What's the matter with you, man, are you crazy? Can't you answer a civil question? [*Gives* ISAAC *a strong slap over the knee.*] Answer me, I say!

ISAAC [*his body twitches with pain; he speaks with ill-disguised anger*]. Let me alone. You could have asked her if you . . .

ORKE. This fellow's too insolent.

ISAAC. And don't get so familiar with me, either, and keep your hands off my knee.

ORKE. Altogether too insolent.

BERRE and MICHEL [*motion to* ORKE *to keep quiet*].

MALKE. I know his neighbors very well. The two sisters Hinde and Sozye — you know them too, Temme — are rather good-looking. But that other one, Gelye, I can't stand at all. A big mouth . . .

ORKE. A lot she knows about looks. [To MALKE.] Do you call yourself good-looking?

MALKE. Gelye has a face dotted with freckles. Isn't that so, Temme?

TEMME. Why, certainly. Just covered with them.

ZELIG. He overlooked the freckles.

ORKE. Bah! A lot they both know what they're talking about! You can take my word for it that . . .

MALKE. Now I'll admit that Hinde and Sozye are really good-looking girls.

ORKE. I say we ought to be more frequent visitors to Isaac's place.

ZELIG [*to* ISAAC]. Why don't you give a ball? . . .

ORKE. In honor of the machine you didn't make.

MICHEL [*angrily*]. What? What? What? It's not right to tease him so. [*Shrugs his shoulders.*]

ZELIG. And invite all of us.

BERRE. You clown, stop your antics.

ORKE. What's it your business? Do your work! What do you care?

BERRE and MICHEL [*make gestures of despair*].

ISAAC [*with suppressed feeling*]. I ask no one to take my part.— [*The office bell rings.* ORKE *runs into the office.*]

SILENCE

BERRE [*sarcastically*]. There's a son for you!

MICHEL [*the same*]. A crackerjack!

MALKE [*laughing*]. And Gelye is to his taste! With that big mouth of hers, and her freckles. A lean, lanky . . . Now the two sisters *are* really . . .

ZELIG. I'll bet he likes all three of 'em.

SENDER. You took the words out of my mouth.

HILYE. Let's leave it to Isaac. Eh, Isaac? What do you say? You'll talk to *us*, won't you? Eh? How? It's a very important question.

MICHEL. Enough of your tomfoolery and your teasing. Enough! He too! Orke's chum! [*Silence. Soon* ZELIG, SENDER, MALKE, TEMME *and* YOSHKE *com-*

mence to sing at their work, all humming different tunes.]

SENDER. Isaac, here comes your wife.

MALKE [*goes to the window*]. Yes. Here she comes. And she's carrying . . .

ZELIG [*sticks* MALKE *with the point of a needle and jumps back to his seat*].

MALKE. Ow! [*Looks around.*] Who stuck me then, eh? — I can tell it was Zelig. [*Begins to hit him.*]

ZELIG [*defending himself*]. Who? Who? I didn't do it!

BAYLYE [*comes in. She is carrying a pot tied about with a sheet that is wet from the contents. To her "Good day," the men and women reply variously, "Good year," "Good day," "Bon jour."*]

ISAAC *and* HILYE [*silent*].

BAYLYE [*going over to* ISAAC]. Here, I brought you dinner. Eat, now. Do you hear? — [*Bitterly.*] Take it, and eat.— [*More bitterly.*] Enough of your obstinacy.

ISAAC [*quietly*]. I don't want to eat.

BAYLYE [*despairingly*]. What do you mean, you don't want to eat? Where are you going to get strength to work?

TEMME. Did he really leave the house without eating his dinner?

BAYLYE. Yes. Without dinner! And do you think he ate anything before dinner-time? He got up at daybreak and went right to work, on that unlucky machine of his, and hasn't had a thing in his mouth since. [*To* ISAAC, *with tears.*] Here, eat something!

BERRE. Don't be childish, Isaac. Eat. What do you call this, anyway? It's foolish.

BAYLYE [*weeping*]. It's been like this for the past three days: He hasn't slept, he hasn't eaten; every moment was given to that unlucky machine of his. [*To* Isaac.] Will you eat or not?

Isaac [*as before*]. I don't want to eat.

Baylye [*to the workers*]. There! Say yourself: how is a woman to endure all this? [*Wailing.*] I can't stand it! I can't stand it!

Malke. What do you care if he doesn't eat? Pff! A lot I'd care!

Baylye. How can a person refuse to eat all day?

Berre [*lays aside his work, goes over to* Isaac *and takes him by the hand*]. Don't be foolish, Isaac. Drop your work, wash up and eat.

Isaac. Please don't bother me. I can't eat.

Berre. What do you mean,—"can't eat"? What kind of words are those? Send for a schnapps — take a little brandy and that'll give you an appetite. Here, Yoshke, bring him a schnapps.

Baylye [*restraining her tears*]. Yes, send for a schnapps.

Isaac. I haven't any money and I don't care for any schnapps.

Berre. It doesn't need much money. I suppose some one of us can advance it. Have you any change about you, Reb Michel?

Michel [*shrugging his shoulders*]. Not a kopeck.

Zelig [*turns his pockets inside out and whistles, touching* Hilye *with his foot*]. You've got some, haven't you?

Hilye. How do you know? Have you been in my pockets?

Leivik. I can lend you the price, Isaac. [*Takes out a rouble.*] I can lend you the whole rouble.

Baylye [*takes the rouble from him; to* Isaac]. Shall I send after a schnapps for you?

BERRE. There's no need of asking. Here, Yoshke, run over and get half a pint.

YOSHKE [*lazily takes the money*]. Smirnóvka?

BERRE. Let it be *Smirnóvka*. But make it quick. [*Pushes YOSHKE out, and speaks in a pleased manner.*] There, that's more like it. You'll have a drink,— it'll cheer you up and then you'll eat. [*Sits down to his work, and speaks with much self-satisfaction.*] A drink is the best remedy. It's the first thing I think of. For this, for that, for headache, for heartache,— a schnapps, and the trouble disappears. [*Turns to* ISAAC.] And don't be a fool. Swallow the whole business at one gulp. You'll eat all the heartier for it.

BAYLYE. He hasn't eaten a thing for almost three days. I don't know what he's lived on.

MALKE. On the machine.

BAYLYE. Yes. The unlucky machine. That's the only explanation.

ZELIG. And what came of it all? Didn't he finish it?

BAYLYE. Finish it? He worked and worked — the whole three days it was impossible to tear him away from the work table, and suddenly he seizes it, smashes it on the floor, and . . .

LEIVIK [*amazed*]. H'm!

BAYLYE. I began to tremble all over,— hands and feet. I shivered like a leaf. And he sat down with staring eyes. . . .

MALKE. An insane man.

LEIVIK. No-o. That's not insanity. It's . . . it's . . .

BAYLYE. What is it then? [*Laughing ironically.*] No. That's not insanity!

ISAAC [*to* BAYLYE]. Do me a favor and go home.

BAYLYE [*looks at him angrily and frightened*]. No. That's not insanity!

BERRE. You really ought to go home. That would make things much better. [*Motions her to leave.* MICHEL *does the same.*]

BAYLYE [*insulted, prepares to go*]. I'm the only one that's ever in his way. [*Angrily.*] Eat, you lunatic!

BERRE. He'll eat. Go home. Don't worry. He'll have a drink and he'll eat.

BAYLYE [*to* ISAAC]. And remember to bring the pot home.

BERRE. All right. He'll bring it.

BAYLYE [*at the door*]. Lunatic! [*Exit.*]

MICHEL. A woman is only a woman after all.

MALKE. I've known Baylye for eight years,— before she was married. My! Wasn't she the lively piece! And now, what a change! She looks something awful!

BERRE. And how did Isaac look eight years ago! To be sure, he always was a queer chap, but outside of that . . .

YOSHKE [*enters with the brandy*].

BERRE [*drops his work, goes to* YOSHKE, *takes the flask from him, together with the change from the rouble, and turns to* ISAAC]. Here. Just swallow some of this brandy and then eat a bite and you'll feel like a new man,— the Isaac you used to be. [*Takes down a glass from the shelf.*] Maybe you've forgotten the old-time Isaac. Let me recall him, then. Do you remember, just outside the city in Korobanovka? [*Pours out a glassful, looking enviously at the flowing brandy.*] Do you remember how you used to . . . Here . . . take . . . Well? Here, take it. . . . [*Puts down the flask, takes* ISAAC's *hat and puts it on his head.*] Well, go to it. Say the blessing and drink it down. [*Takes the flask again.*] Take it, Isaac. Don't be a child. Here, Isaac.

MICHEL. Bah! Isaac! Don't be obstinate. Drink it down and eat your dinner. Why are you acting so foolishly, eh?

BERRE [*bringing the glass to* ISAAC's *lips*]. Drink, I tell you! Chump!

ZELIG [*to* ISAAC]. Better take it quickly or he'll drink it himself!

ISAAC [*he tries to turn his head away. Suddenly he seizes the glass and empties it at a single gulp*].

BERRE [*follows the disappearing brandy with envious eyes. He smacks his lips, and makes a wry face, as if he had felt the coolness and the bitter taste of the brandy*]. Now you're acting sensibly. That's the way I like to see you. [*Takes the empty glass from* ISAAC.] And now another one. [*Pours another glass, sniffing it as he does so.*] No waiting, either.

ISAAC [*restraining* BERRE's *hand. Sinister*]. Give me the flask. [*Takes the flask out of* BERRE's *hand, puts it to his lips and swallows the entire contents at one gulp.*]

BERRE [*who has given the flask unwillingly, follows every movement of* ISAAC's, *stretching his neck forward as he does so. After* ISAAC *has emptied the flask, he takes it from him and offers him the glass*]. And now take the little bit that's left in the glass, and make it a full measure. You refuse? Then now for your dinner. [*Puts down the glass and the flask, and shoves forward the pot and the bread.*] Now, eat your dinner.

ISAAC [*leans with both arms against the loom, and hides his face in his hands*].

BERRE. Eat, Isaac. Eat. And don't waste any time about it. It's cold already.

ISAAC [*places his head on his left arm*].

BERRE. What have you lain down for? I tell you, take your dinner. [*Tries to raise his head.*]

ISAAC [*thrusts him aside with his right hand*].

BERRE [*insulted*]. Very well, then. Lie there. I tell you to eat. If you don't want to, all right. Do as you please. [*Takes the flask and looks regretfully at it. Then he casts envious eyes upon the glass.*]

HILYE. Well, Berre! Here's your health!

BERRE. Don't eat, then. I won't bother with you any longer. [*Goes back to his place.*]

LEIVIK. Why don't you eat, Isaac? You must have something solid in your stomach.

BERRE [*indignant*]. I never saw such an obstinate mule in all my days.

ZELIG. I'll bet he'll fall asleep altogether.

MICHEL. Let him sleep, then. That's the best thing for him.

BERRE. Ah-h! I know whenever I take a swallow of brandy. . . . I . . . I . . . I become a new man entirely. And maybe Isaac wasn't a drinker in his day! Hm! I don't know what's come over him.

LEIVIK [*to* ZELIG]. Is he really sleeping, Zelig?

ZELIG. I think so. [*Shakes* ISAAC.] Are you asleep, Isaac?

LEIVIK. You clown!

HILYE [*singing*]. "Sleep, little birdie, close your sweet eyes. . . ."

MICHEL. There's a crowd for you!

TEMME. His dinner will get cold. [*Arising.*] I'll take it down to Ida's and put it into her oven.

ISAAC [*sits up and takes out his handkerchief*].

TEMME [*frightened*]. Look. He's been crying! [LEIVIK, BERRE, ZELIG *and* MALKE *jump up from their places with an exclamation:* "*Crying!*" *They come over to* ISAAC *and look upon him with deep concern.*]

MICHEL [*shakes his head and speaks in a tone of bitter disgust*]. Crying!

HILYE and SENDER [*look with curiosity towards* ISAAC, *but remain in their places, continuing their work*].

YOSHKE [*comes from his table and looks with curiosity at* ISAAC].

BERRE. You're no kind of man at all, Isaac. Pooh! Upon my word. If I knew that, I certainly wouldn't have urged you to drink. Really, you're no kind of man at all.

HILYE. Let him go home and sleep it off.

BERRE. That's a good idea. Go home and sleep it off. What are you crying about? Pooh! Upon my word it's a shame and a disgrace. Take my advice and go home. So you won't work to-day, either. Imagine you're still at your invention. Go on home. Here.... Here's the rest of the rouble. Take it. See? I'm putting it into your pocket. Are there any holes in your pocket? [*Feels* ISAAC'S *pocket.*] No holes. Now go home.

ISAAC [*sinks forward on his arms again. His whole body is convulsed with his quiet weeping*].

LEIVIK. Really, Isaac, you're . . .

BERRE. It's the first time in my life that I see anything like this.

HILYE [*to* SENDER]. Look, will you! Temme is crying, too!

TEMME [*drying her eyes*]. Hilye, you've got a heart of stone.

LEIVIK [*coming over to* ISAAC]. Isaac. It's a shame. . . . Really. . . .

ISAAC. Let me alone. . . . Let me be. . . . I must . . . I must . . .

BERRE [*coming over to* ISAAC]. What must you,

what? You mustn't anything. Did you ever hear the like? He *must* cry!

ISAAC [*angrily*]. Let me alone!

BERRE [*with a deprecatory gesture*]. You see. It's like dealing with a madman. [*The workers return to their places.*]

LEIVIK [*sadly*]. H'm!

BERRE. It's the first time in my life that . . .

MALKE. Bah! I don't like to see a man cry.

ZELIG [*moved*]. The poor fellow!

TEMME [*takes the pot and goes out*].

SILENCE

ISAAC [*gradually stops weeping and finally is silent. The workers glance often in his direction*].

GOLDIN [*enters. Walks over to* ISAAC *and makes a gesture of astonishment*]. What's he lying there for, I'd like to know!

MALKE. He's just been crying.

GOLDIN. Crying? What do you mean, he's been crying? Because his machine was a failure? [*Waking* ISAAC.] Say, Isaac. What were you crying about? Wake up! [*Notices the brandy flask.*] Who's been drinking here? Was it Isaac?

MALKE. He hasn't eaten anything all day long, so they told him to take some brandy for an appetizer.

GOLDIN. In plain words, then, he got drunk. Bah! First you couldn't get him to move from his house, because he was fussing around a machine of his. And now, when he finally does come back to work, he gets as soused as a pig and falls asleep.

ISAAC [*moves nervously, raises his head and lets it fall immediately*].

GOLDIN. If you're drunk, go home and sleep it off

there. I don't need any drunkards around here.— Where's Temme?

Isaac [*slowly arising*]. Are you angry because I didn't bring you a third machine?

Goldin. You pig, you! You and your machines can go to the devil together! Where's Temme, I say?

Malke. Isaac's wife was here and brought him his dinner. And Temme took the pot to Ida's, so that it shouldn't get cold.

Goldin. And hasn't she anything else to do besides warming his pots?

Isaac. And if I'd have brought you the machine you wouldn't be so angry now. [*Enter* Temme.]

Goldin. Where've you been? Eh? It's your business to sit and work,— not take care of his pots! I don't pay you or anybody else to be his servant.

Isaac [*scarcely able to restrain his anger*]. I didn't ask her.

Temme. It didn't take more than a minute. His dinner would have got cold.

Goldin. Not even a second. Let him eat it cold or not eat it at all. It's none of your concern. You're supposed to sit and work.

Isaac. Is that how deeply interested you were in my machine?

Goldin [*furious*]. To the devil with you and your machines — I've told you once already. Now,— do you understand? For all I care you may . . .

Orke [*comes running in*]. What's all the hollering about?

Goldin. He comes here, gets dead drunk . . .

Isaac [*banging his fist against the loom*]. Stop that talk about "drunk," I tell you! Do you understand me or not?

GOLDIN [*his mouth agape with astonishment. All work comes to a standstill*].

ORKE. My! My! The fellow's really angry!

ISAAC. Don't talk to me about getting drunk. Talk to your own son.

GOLDIN. You brazen-faced fool! You insolent pig!

MICHEL and BERRE [*surround* GOLDIN].

LEIVIK and ZELIG [*hold* ISAAC *back*].

MICHEL. Stop it, Notte,—can't you see what a fuss you're starting?

LEIVIK. Calm yourself, calm yourself, Isaac.

ORKE [*to* ISAAC]. You needn't drag me into this.

BERRE. Orke . . ah! . . Have some common sense. . .

LEIVIK [*to* ISAAC]. Calm yourself. Calm yourself.

GOLDIN [*to* ISAAC]. You're through working here.

ISAAC. You bet I am. But before I go, you'll please give me back my press and my braiding-machine.

ORKE [*putting his hands to his ears. Mockingly*]. What? Give you back what? I didn't hear that. Repeat that, please.

GOLDIN. Your press and your machine? You were well paid for them.

ISAAC [*makes a threatening motion.* LEIVIK *and* ZELIG *hold him back*].

ZELIG. Calm. Be calm.

GOLDIN. The nerve of the man to want back his machines! His, he calls them. I paid you for them, and they're mine, not yours.

ORKE. *His* press and *his* machine! Such wonderful inventions, such marvelous brain-products! You can see what you're good for. Fussed and fussed around for three days. . . .

ISAAC. "Marvelous brain-products"— Can you do better?

ORKE. Pff! But where's your new machine?

ISAAC. I'm asking you. Can you do better?

ORKE. And I'm asking you: where's your new machine?

GOLDIN. What are you wasting words with him for? Here, Yoshke. Run over and call Shmerel. Tell him the job's open for him, and that he can come to work right away. And enough of this talk.

YOSHKE [*reluctantly prepares to go*].

ISAAC [*arises, snatches his coat and walks slowly towards the door, accompanied by* LEIVIK *and* ZELIG, *who are calming him. Suddenly he rushes upon the press, lifts it in the air, throws himself upon the machine and smashes it under his feet so that its parts fly in all directions*]. Now I can leave! . . . Now I can leave. . . . [LEIVIK *and* ZELIG *and* BERRE *try to restrain him from breaking the machines.*]

GOLDIN. Call the police! Police! Orke, run for a policeman!

ORKE. Hilye, run for a policeman!

ISAAC [*still stepping upon parts of the machines and smashing them*]. Now I can leave! [*Tears himself out of the men's hands and walks through the door as calmly as possible.*]

GOLDIN *and* ORKE [*rush after him. They are held back*].

GOLDIN. Call a policeman, I say! Call the police!

ISAAC [*from the yard*]. Take this! [*A stone comes crashing through the window, smashes all the panes and hits* ORKE *in the side. A cry of "Oh!" arises from all the bystanders*].

ORKE. He's killed me!

GOLDIN. Call the police! Police!

CURTAIN

ACT III

ISAAC's *cellar-dwelling. It is late night, of the same day as the two previous acts. On the table burns a lamp, whose glass chimney is thickly covered with soot. The room is half dark. Only shadows, black silhouettes, are visible.*

GISHINKE [*sits in the forward bed, crying*]. Ma! Ma!
PINYE [*standing close to her, muttering*]. Dead. Dead.
GISHINKE [*crossly*]. She didn't die! Ma isn't dead! You're dead!
PINYE. Everything is dead. Dead.
GISHINKE [*crying louder*]. No. She isn't dead!
PINYE. Dead. Dead. Heaven. Earth. And God. And God. Buried in the dead heaven. Covered with the dead earth. And everything is cold and dark. And cold. And dark. . . .
GISHINKE. Ma-a-a-ma! Where is mamma?
PINYE. Dead. All are dead.
GISHINKE [*at the top of her lungs*]. No! She isn't dead! She isn't dead! Mamma isn't dead! [GELYE *enters from her room. Soon after her comes* HINDE *from her room. Both wear nightgowns and are wrapped in large shawls.*]
GELYE [*to* PINYE]. What are you standing there for scaring the life out of her? Go over to your place.

[*To* GISHINKE.] Don't cry, Gishinke. Your mother will soon be back.

PINYE [*walks back slowly to his place and sits down. From time to time he utters strange, tearful sobs*].

HINDE. What's the kid bawling about?

GISHINKE. Where's my mamma?

GELYE. The old lunatic came over to her. . . .

GISHINKE. She didn't die, did she?

GELYE [*continuing*]. . . . And . . .

HINDE [*to* GISHINKE]. Your mamma'll soon be here.

GELYE. The poor child's crying her eyes out.

HINDE. Something must have happened to Isaac. Goldin must have had him arrested. But why doesn't Baylye come back?

GISHINKE [*crying*]. Mamma isn't coming.

GELYE. Go to sleep, Gishinke. Your mamma'll be right back. We'll sit down near you. All right?

GISHINKE. I want my mamma.

GELYE [*wrapping the bedclothes about* GISHINKE *and sitting down beside her*]. There. Quiet. That's a good girl. We'll sit right near you. See? Hinde has sat down, too. And your mamma'll be here right away.

HINDE. Sleep, Gishinke, sleep.

GISHINKE [*a trifle reassured*]. Mamma hasn't died.

GELYE. What put that into your head? Of course your mother hasn't died.

GISHINKE. Hasn't died?

GELYE. No, no. You silly little girl. Your mamma hasn't died. Go to sleep.

HINDE. The old fellow makes everybody sick with his eternal chatter about dead heavens and dead earths.

GISHINKE. And my papa hasn't died, either?

GELYE. Sleep. Sleep, Gishinke. Nobody has died.

HINDE. Who can tell what's happened to Isaac?

Haven't you heard what took place in the factory to-day? He had a fit of crying.

GELYE. They got him drunk first.

GISHINKE. When'll mamma come?

GELYE. Soon. Soon. Fall asleep, now.

HINDE. . . . And he smashed his press and the braiding-machine.

SOZYE [*enters in petticoat and jacket, her hands folded across her bosom. She feels very cold*]. Well? What's the news? [*Walks over to the bed.*] Oh! This is Gelye! I thought you were talking to Baylye here. Hasn't Baylye come back yet?

GELYE. Neither Baylye nor Isaac.

SOZYE. That's very strange.

GISHINKE [*to* SOZYE]. Mamma hasn't died.

HINDE. My! What a time they had there!

GISHINKE [*to* SOZYE]. And papa hasn't died, either.

GELYE. Sleep. Sleep. If you don't go to sleep, we'll go away and leave you all alone.

GISHINKE. No. Don't go 'way.

GELYE. Then go to sleep. [*Runs her hand through* GISHINKE'S *hair and hums a lullaby.*]

HINDE. It must have been terrible there. He took a big stone and smashed a couple of window panes. . . .

SOZYE. Are you talking about Isaac?

GELYE. That's why I reckon that Goldin has certainly had him locked up.

HINDE. It's quite likely. They must have caught him in the streets.

SOZYE [*shivering*]. Brrr! How that son of his came running here with a policeman, and searched our room. . . .

GELYE. Ours too.

HINDE. I shivered all over, like a leaf.

GELYE. I wanted to throw something in his face. . . .
HINDE. The fop!
GELYE. The loafer!
HINDE. The cheap sport! Clean shaven, curled mustache, his hat on one side, rings on his fingers. . . .
SOZYE [*shivering*]. And the way he dresses!
GELYE. This morning, when we left the house together, he simply insisted that I tell him where I was going, and that I let him carry my bundle . . . and he asked what I do, and where I usually go walking . . .
HINDE. Do you think he's handsome? I don't take him for a good-looking fellow, at all. His eyes are so . . .
GELYE. . . . And he asked where I go walking, and with whom. And he made such queer motions, and bows. . . . [*Mocking* ORKE.] This way, and that way. . . .
SOZYE [*to* HINDE]. Do you know whom he looks like?
HINDE [*after a moment's thought*]. Whom?
SOZYE. Like Kopelyovitz.
HINDE. What? Not in the least. Kopelyovitz is taller, and has blond hair. . . .
SOZYE. Yes, but . . . His lips . . . his nose . . .
HINDE. You're 'way off. You don't know what you're talking about.
SOZYE. . . . He escorted me up to Vichman's door. . . . I was bringing something to Vichman's, you know . . . and he took me right up to Vichman's door; I simply couldn't get rid of him.
HINDE. And with all his other virtues, he's such a coarse fellow too.
SOZYE. Yes. And he mentions such improper things.
GELYE. He said nothing improper to me. He'd have caught it from me if he ever dared. But he kept paying such exaggerated compliments. [*Mocking* ORKE.]

This way, and that way. "You're such a clever young lady, and so . . ." [*There is a knocking at the outer door. She jumps to her feet.*]

HINDE. It's Baylye, I guess.

SOZYE [*shivering with the cold, she goes to open the door*]. Brrr. . . . Brrr. . . .

HINDE. I'm terrible anxious to know what's happening to Isaac.

SOZYE [*crying out*]. Oh!

ZELIG [*in the entry*]. Don't be scared. I called to see whether Isaac has come home yet.

SOZYE [*comes back into the room*].

ZELIG [*following her. He wears a black coat*].

GELYE and HINDE [*hurriedly put their hair and clothes in order. The three girls, attempting to hide their partial undress, come close together*].

ZELIG. Is he here already?

HINDE. No. Not yet.

GELYE. And Baylye isn't here yet, either.

ZELIG. She must still be looking for him. I went to several of his friends, looked through quite a few streets — but he's not to be heard or seen.

GELYE. If he hasn't been arrested, I'm afraid he's done something desperate to himself.

SOZYE. Goldin's son was here with a policeman.

ZELIG. I know. Maybe we didn't do our best to hold him back!

HINDE. Came dashing in here. [*Imitating* ORKE.] "Where is he? Produce Isaac at once! I'll . . ."

SOZYE. And then he searched the whole place for him.

ZELIG. Orke wanted to show off. [*Imitating* ORKE's *voice.*] "Where is he? I want him!"

SOZYE [*to the others*]. Yes! That's just how he hollered!

ZELIG. I know him inside out. [*Imitating* ORKE's *motions.*] "Where is he? Produce Isaac at once! I must have him! . . ." [*All laugh.*]

SOZYE [*to the others*]. That's Orke to a dot!

ZELIG. He was here early this morning, too, wasn't he?

GELYE [*with an ironic gesture, and pressing her lips together*]. We had the honor.

ZELIG. And he went walking with one of you.

GELYE [*same as before, and with mock pride*]. With myself.

SOZYE [*to the others*]. Goodness! But how news does spread!

ZELIG. And he's already been talking about being a more frequent visitor hereabouts.

HINDE. As if we haven't enough troubles already.

GELYE [*ironically*]. We need him badly.

ZELIG. But isn't he a handsome chap?

GELYE. A regular picture!

HINDE. Ugh! Such queer eyes.

ZELIG. And yet he's so popular with the girls.

GELYE [*shaking her head and pressing her lips together*]. H'mm! You don't say!

HINDE. He?!

SOZYE [*looks at the other girls and laughs in surprise*].

GELYE. He insisted on accompanying me through the streets, and I just couldn't get rid of him.

ZELIG [*shaking his head*]. Oh! Orke, Orke! Bad luck to you!

SOZYE. I could swear that somebody's at the door. [*The door is pushed open from outside.*]

ZELIG. Yes. Somebody's there. [*They take a few steps towards the door.*]

BERRE [*enters. He wears an expression of dejection and worry, as if he felt guilty of what had happened.*]

ZELIG. Why! It's Berre!

BERRE. Zelig! [*Looks about him.*] Is Isaac here already?

ZELIG. Neither Isaac nor his wife.

BERRE. She must be running all around the town. And he isn't here? He must be somewhere, sleeping off his spree.

ZELIG. Unless Goldin has had him arrested.

BERRE. About two hours ago, around nine o'clock, he was at Rivve Shaynin's tavern.

ZELIG. How did you learn that?

BERRE. I was looking for him high and low, so I went to Rivve Shaynin's tavern, too.

HINDE. That's at the other end of the town, if I'm not mistaken.

ZELIG [*Hitting* BERRE *over the shoulder*]. I guess Berre knows where all the taverns are.

BERRE. Clown! I went in to see whether Isaac was there.— And he had really been there, stayed a couple of hours, didn't say a word to anybody, and drank down one glass after another. They say he sat there in such a rage that everybody took him for a madman. He left the place dead drunk. Where he went, nobody knows.

ZELIG. I'll bet he's lying in some ditch.

HINDE [*coquettishly*]. Ugh!

SOZYE [*with a shudder*]. Brrr!

ZELIG. Are you folks cold?

SOZYE. Just a strange feeling. . . . Brrr!

ZELIG. A young girl ought never to be cold.

HINDE. She's always freezing.

SOZYE. I don't know. I feel so queer. . . . Brrr!

BERRE [*who has been standing absorbed in thought,*

his gaze upon the floor]. I really don't know where else I can hunt for him. I went to several other taverns. . . .

ZELIG. That's understood.

BERRE [*scornfully*]. Tfu! You clown! [*The outer door is opened.*]

BAYLYE [*comes running in*]. What! He is already here? [*She sees at once that* ISAAC *is not there.*] Not here yet? [*Bursting into tears.*] I'm sure he's done something desperate to himself. O, God in Heaven, what a misfortune has . . .

HINDE. At nine o'clock he was seen at Rivve Shaynin's tavern.

BERRE. Yes. Nine o'clock. And he left the place dead drunk. Where he went to, I don't know. I've been hunting for him all night.

ZELIG. I, too. But the city's an awful big place.

BAYLYE [*her voice choked with tears*]. I searched everywhere. And I made a terrible scene at the Goldins' home. I threw myself on the floor and begged them to give me back Isaac, to tell me where he was. Mrs. Goldin swore by her life that they hadn't had him arrested. [*Moaning, wringing her hands.*] Oh, I know he has committed something desperate. How can I bear it all?

GELYE. No. Not that. He must be lying somewhere, drunk.

HINDE. In some gutter.

SOZYE. Brrr!

BAYLYE [*lamenting*]. Unhappy woman that I am! That I should have lived to see this day!

BERRE. They told me there that he was dead drunk — that he could barely stand on his feet.

BAYLYE [*as before*]. Oh! Woe is me! . . . And he borrowed a rouble, too.

BERRE. And it was I who put the change in his pocket. If I had foreseen such an outcome . . .

ZELIG. You'd have put it into your own pocket.

BERRE [*angrily*]. For shame. Clown! Nothing but his jokes for any occasion at all. [ZELIG, SOZYE, *and* HINDE *laugh.*]

BAYLYE [*hysterical, running about the room*]. Oh! May flames consume Rivve Shaynin and her tavern together. May all trace of her be wiped out in a single night. When she sees that a Jew wants to get drunk, she shouldn't sell him any liquor.

GELYE. Much the tavern-keeper cares who wants to get drunk.

HINDE. Little difference it makes,— whether it's a Jew or a Gentile.

ZELIG. As long as he has the price or something to pawn — Eh, Berre?

BERRE [*angrily*]. There's no being serious with you! [ZELIG, HINDE *and* SOZYE *laugh.*]

BAYLYE [*as before*]. Where shall I look for him now? Where can I even begin to hunt for him? Where can I even begin to hunt for him? [*Wailing.*] I can't stand it any longer. Suicide is the only way out. Good God in Heaven! [*The outer door is opened. All move toward the door. Enter* LEIVIK *and* SENDER.]

LEIVIK. Well? Is he already here?

BAYLYE. Not at all! May he so dwell among the living. . . .

LEIVIK. Petrush, the watchman, told me that this afternoon, around two or three o'clock, he saw a young man in the woods. He says the fellow ran about wildly, beat the tree trunks with his fists, tore the bark from them, bit them, and struck his head against them. According to his description, I think it was Isaac.

BAYLYE [*bringing her hands to her head*]. He's surely gone mad. Oh! Oh!

LEIVIK. So I called Sender, and we both went to the woods, to the place where the watchman said he saw him. But we found nobody.

SENDER. I claimed beforehand that our going was useless. A fine chance you've got to find a person in the woods,— especially at night.

LEIVIK. Just the same I'd have kept on searching. By the light of the moon. . . .

SENDER. Then why didn't you remain there?

HINDE. At nine o'clock this evening he was at Rivve Shaynin's tavern.

BERRE. Well. That's right near the woods.

BAYLYE [*weeping*]. Then he must certainly have gone back into the woods. How can we look for him? How shall we find him?

ZELIG. You'll find him dead drunk. Berre says that he was barely able to stand on his feet.

BERRE. *I* didn't see him. That's merely what I was told.

BAYLYE. Where can we look for him? Where can we find him?

HINDE. Maybe he really went back into the woods.

BAYLYE. He got drunk and did violence to himself. [*Wailing.*] What's to be done? What can we even begin to do? Let's be off to the woods.

SENDER. Ha! You talk like a child. Think of her wanting to hunt for a person in the woods, at night. And here we are, just coming from the woods ourselves.

LEIVIK. We could all go.

ZELIG [*to the girls*]. Do you want to come to the woods?

HINDE and SOZYE [*look at* GELYE, *to see what she thinks of the proposal*].

GELYE. It's a useless task. The trouble will be in vain.

BERRE. That's so. Where can we go, for instance?

SENDER. And here we've just come from there, too.

ZELIG [*nudges* SENDER *significantly, and nods his head in the direction of the girls*].

SENDER [*with a wry face*]. Ow!

BAYLYE [*wrings her hands*]. What's to be done? What can we begin to do? What can we begin to do?

BERRE. He'll sleep it off somewhere, I tell you, and then come home.

GELYE. And who knows whether it was really Isaac that the watchman saw in the woods?

LEIVIK. It was, according to Petrush's description. Middle height. Blond beard. Derby.

SENDER. There's a description for you! Is he the only man that's of middle height and that wears a derby?

BAYLYE [*running about*]. What's to be done? Where can we look? Where can we find him? [*Sits down upon the further bed and weeps.*]

SILENCE

SENDER [*whispers something to* LEIVIK, *indicating the girls.* LEIVIK *listens, distraught*].

ZELIG [*to the girls*]. An awful night, isn't it?

GELYE [*sighing*]. Yes. A night of horrors.

HINDE. Ah! Such a night.

SOZYE [*shivering*]. Brrr!

ZELIG [*to* LEIVIK *and* SENDER]. Did you ever know a young lady as cold as this one?

SENDER. It's really an awful pity.—
[*Pause.* BAYLYE's *weeping is heard.* BERRE *stands scratching his beard.* SENDER *and* ZELIG *stand opposite the girls. They would like to open a conversation with them, and the girls are expecting it. Meanwhile the girls seek the best poses they can assume, and cast sympathetic glances towards* BAYLYE. LEIVIK, *too, looks at the girls, but something is on his mind.*]

ZELIG [*to the girls*]. I was telling Isaac to-day to give a ball here and to invite us.

BAYLYE. You see the kind of a ball he's given. [*Weeps louder.*]

HINDE. What do you mean? Why should he give a ball? [ZELIG *laughs and looks at* SENDER. GELYE *shakes her head disapprovingly, and turns away.*]

SENDER [*to* ZELIG *and* LEIVIK, *nodding towards* GELYE]. She understands why, I'll wager.

GELYE [*as before*]. Little enough to understand.

LEIVIK. I'm wondering and wondering where we can look for him.

BERRE. There's nothing left to do now. We'll have to wait till to-morrow morning. That's all there is to it. And now it's time to go home. [BALYLE *continues to weep. Pause.*] Well, I'm going home. Good night to you all. What's the use of my idling here? Good night, all. [*Exit.*]

ZELIG [*to* SENDER]. Shall we be going, too?

SENDER. What else can we do?

ZELIG. And you, Leivik?

LEIVIK. We'd better go. We can't do anything else now.

ZELIG [*to the girls*]. Well, as hard as it is for me to tear myself away . . .

BERRE [*his voice is heard from the street*]. Isaac!

Isaac! [*All rush to the door and run outside. The room is left empty, except for the sleeping* GISHINKE *and old* PINYE.]

PINYE [*stands still at the door, and speaks in a moaning tone*]. Desolate! Desolate! [*Moans.*]

ISAAC [*enters, led by* BERRE *and* LEIVIK. *He is still drunk and cannot stand*].

ZELIG [*following them, jumping and clapping his hands*]. He's here! He's here! He's here! He's here! [BAYLYE *comes back.*]

BERRE [*cheered by* ISAAC'S *return, he speaks freely and happily, as if his guilt in* ISAAC'S *spree had been redeemed*]. I go up the cellar-steps and I see somebody standing there,— leaning against the wall. One of his hands here, the other there,— and he is staring at the moon,— like this. I take another look: it's Isaac!

ISAAC [*in a drunken, dejected voice*]. What are you so happy about?

BERRE. Happy about? Why, man, we've been looking for you all night. And there he was, standing like this, staring at the . . .

BAYLYE. Where've you been wandering, drunk as you are?

ISAAC. I'm no longer there.

BERRE. I take a look. . . . Who can be standing there, I ask myself. . . .

BAYLYE [*to* ISAAC]. I'll grab hold of something and split your head open. I'll pour out all the bitterness of my heart on to your head,— your whole body and soul. . . . [*They try to quiet her.*]

BERRE. But, no, ha-ha. . . . I go up nearer to him — Lord of the Universe, who can it be standing like that, at night, I ask myself. So I go up nearer to him. . . .

BAYLYE. I'll teach him to borrow roubles, and spend them getting drunk! [BERRE *angrily motions her to keep quiet.* BAYLYE *sits down upon the further bed, weeps and mumbles to herself, every now and then breaking into a curse.*

LEIVIK [*to* ISAAC]. Were you in the woods?

ISAAC [*drops suddenly upon the chair near the bureau and bursts into tears*].

ZELIG [*to the girls*]. He cried to-day in the factory, too.

BAYLYE. Let him cry for his brains, and his wasted days and years. His machine is dearer to him than his wife and children.

TSIPPE [*appears at her door, only half awake*]. What's the matter?

GELYE [*hastens to her*]. Nothing. Nothing.

TSIPPE. Has he come already? Is that he crying? What's he crying about?

GELYE [*pushing her back into the room*]. Nothing, I told you. Nothing. You'll know all about it to-morrow. Go to sleep.

TSIPPE. And why are you still up? It must be late.

GELYE. Go, I'll soon come.

TSIPPE. What's this crowd here for? A regular wedding.

GELYE [*fast losing her patience*]. What are you standing there for, scratching yourself? [*Pushes her back into the room, and closes the door.*]

TSIPPE [*behind the door*]. What are you pushing me about for? Hey?

GELYE [*returns to her place.* SENDER *and* ZELIG *smile at her*].

ISAAC [*raising his hands above his head*]. How unhappy I feel! How unhappy! How unhappy! . . .

BAYLYE. He feels unhappy! May unhappiness blight his whole life! Goes and gets drunk. . . .

ISAAC. Leivik, I feel unhappy! Un-hap-py! [*Rubs his chest.*]

LEIVIK. Why, Isaac! You're acting just like a child!

BERRE. In all my life I've never seen such a person!

ISAAC. Leivik, I am wretched.

LEIVIK. What do you mean, wretched? Don't be foolish.

SENDER. Don't be a chump, and go to bed.

SOZYE [*shivering*]. That's really the best thing to do.

ISAAC. I feel wretched, Leivik.— Even you don't understand me.

LEIVIK. I understand you very well.

BAYLYE [*sarcastically*]. He's so deep, you've got to study to understand him!

ISAAC. I feel wretched, Leivik.— I was in the woods. I was there . . .

LEIVIK. Petrush, the watchman told me that he had seen you there. We've been hunting for you all night long.

BAYLYE. He wasn't worth the trouble. The drunkard!

BERRE [*motioning her to keep silent*]. Well, I'm going home now. Time to go to bed. Who's coming along? Nobody? Then I'll go myself. Good night. I advise all of you to go home and leave him alone to sleep it off! That's the best thing. Well. Good night. [*Exit.*]

LEIVIK. I guess I'll be going, too. Undress, Isaac, and lie down to sleep.

ISAAC [*seizing* LEIVIK'*s hand*]. I feel wretched. I feel wretched. [LEIVIK *looks at the others, and shrugs his shoulders.*]

ZELIG [*to the girls*]. I don't feel a bit sleepy. In fact, I'd enjoy a nice walk now. It's such a beautiful night. Who'll come along?

GELYE. Not I. I'd prefer to go to sleep. Good night, everybody. [*Runs into her room.*]

ZELIG and SENDER [*bowing*]. Good night, mademoiselle!

ZELIG. And remember to dream of me. [*To* HINDE *and* SOZYE.] Well, what do you say? [SOZYE *looks to* HINDE *for a reply.*]

HINDE [*to* SOZYE]. Do you want to go?

SOZYE. Trifle too late, isn't it?

HINDE. Well, then we'll go to sleep, too. Good night.

SENDER. We, also.

ZELIG. Are you going to stay, Leivik?

LEIVIK [*shows his hand, which* ISAAC *still clutches, and shrugs his shoulders*].

[SENDER *and* ZELIG, HINDE *and* SOZYE, *go to the outer door, where they stand chatting and laughing, out of view.*]

BAYLYE [*arises, going over to the forward bed and bringing the cradle near to it. She turns down the wick of the lamp, takes off her shoes, places the sleeping* GISHINKE *nearer to the wall, gets into bed and covers herself*].

LEIVIK. Lie down to sleep, Isaac. Go to bed.

ISAAC. My heart is heavy. My heart is heavy.

BAYLYE. Sober up and it'll feel light again.

ISAAC. I was in the woods. I went there right from the factory. You know I didn't really want to go there. But I went, I had to go, Something made me go,—made me rush onward, onward, onward.

BAYLYE. Say yourself: isn't he talking like a madman?

LEIVIK. You shouldn't have drunk the brandy that Berre gave you.

BAYLYE. To borrow money and get drunk on it!

ISAAC. I wouldn't have drunk it. But he brought it close to my nostrils, and the smell of it went to my head, and through all my being, and I had to drink.

BAYLYE. Had to drink! He had to drink! The law forced him to!

LEIVIK. You should have gone home, and to bed.

ISAAC. Something made me rush onward. I dashed through the streets. And I came to the woods. The streets felt so narrow to me. In the streets there was no room to think. Only when I reached the free fields did I myself feel free, and unrestricted. And a heaviness came over my heart. Ah, how heavy, how heavy, how heavy!

BAYLYE [*angrily*]. Go to sleep, and let me sleep, too.

ISAAC. Then only was I able to think, to understand. And I felt it all,— I felt it all! — [*From the outer door comes the sound of laughter.*]

BAYLYE. And those ninnies there are giggling, the . . .

DOBBE [*from her room*]. What's going on there, anyway? Hey? [*The outer door is quickly closed.*]

HINDE [*from the outer room*]. Isaac's come back. . . .

DOBBE [*as before*]. But who just went out? [*Silence.*]

ISAAC. I felt that I was an orphan, after having destroyed my press and my machine.

LEIVIK. Now, aren't you the fool? You'll certainly be able to . . .

ISAAC. And in my heart there was a gnawing misery, because I was so helpless, so helpless, so helpless. Do you understand? I have the will, the vision, but not the ability. I want to do something, you understand, and I can't. And yet, I can! Do you understand,— I *know* that I can. And . . . And . . . And . . . You said today in the factory that sometimes when you see a fine painting, you become so sad, and some one seems to be inside of you, tugging away at your heart, tugging.

LEIVIK. Just the same you see it doesn't unnerve me. It keeps tugging away until it stops. You've got to be a man. . . .

BAYLYE [*turning around so that she faces the wall*]. A fine man *he* is!

ISAAC. I'm a different sort of a person. I raised my hands in the open fields and began to shriek, shriek, shrie-e-ek!

BAYLYE. Shriek your head off! What are you shrieking now for? Let us sleep! He'll wake the children yet.

ISAAC. There was something that I wanted to shriek out of me. Before my eyes stood the press and the braiding-machine, ruined, smashed to bits, wrecked. . . . *My* press, *my* machine.

LEIVIK. Say yourself, Isaac. Aren't you the fool?

ISAAC. But all that is nothing aside of the fact that I can't accomplish the things I feel in me,— I can't, I can't, I can't!

BAYLYE. Please, Leivik, go home. Then he'll go to bed, too.

ISAAC. When I came to the woods I began to beat the trees, to bite them, to tear them, strike my head against them, my hands, my feet. And my heart didn't feel even one hair lighter. I threw myself down on the earth, writhed and tossed about. . . .

LEIVIK. Heavens!

ISAAC. I tore up the grass, bit the earth. And suddenly there rolled out of my pocket a couple of coins.

... [*His speech shows signs of his extreme exhaustion.*] And when I saw the money, I was seized with a desire to drink, drink, drink.

Leivik. Really, I thought more of you than that.

Baylye [*snores, and says something in her sleep*].

Pinye [*arises, and commences to walk about the room*].

Leivik. Well, I'll be going now. And you go to sleep. And be a little bit more of a man. You mustn't lose courage at the very first!

Isaac. The drinking didn't relieve me. It still gnawed and gnawed inside of me. And I roamed through the streets, everywh — and it kept on gnawing, gnawing. Do you understand? There I was, unable to stand on my feet, yet my head was clear.

Leivik. Have a good sleep and you'll wake up a different man in the morning.

Isaac. *You* can sleep off such thoughts. But I — [*Shakes his head.*] No. I'll not sleep mine off. To-morrow, and the next day, and the day after next, I'll be consumed and crazed by the thought that I can't accomplish what I feel in me,— that I can't, I can't. Chains fetter my hands, heavy weights oppress my mind. . . .

Leivik. That's why I'm telling you I thought you had more sense. You know how badly I wanted to become an artist. But I say to myself, "Well, it wasn't to be. That's all. If you can't go over, you've got to go under!"

Isaac. I'm different, I tell you. I'm a different sort of person. No brandy can bring me relief, neither can sleep.

Leivik. That remains to be seen. Just have a good sleep.

Isaac [*arises, uncertain on his feet*]. You see? I can barely stand, you see? Yet inside of me there's that gnawing at my heart, and my mind cannot forget. It's a trifle dizzy, but it cannot forget. [*Takes a few steps toward* Leivik, *wavers, and falls with his head towards the cupboard.*]

Baylye [*aroused by the noise*]. What's the matter? What's the matter?

Leivik. Isaac fell. I'll pick him up and put him to bed.

Baylye [*falling asleep again*]. For my part he may sleep forever.

Isaac. Don't pick me up, Leivik. I feel all right this way. Let me lie. I don't need any bed.

Leivik [*raising him*]. But you can't lie like this all night long.

Isaac. I'll lie right here. Don't pick me up, Leivik. Let the cold earth cool my feverish head. I feel better here.

Leivik. You're crazy. Well, good-night. Who'll close the door?

Isaac. You may leave it open. No thieves will come here.

Leivik. Don't you think I'd better put you into bed?

Isaac. No. I prefer this place. It cools my head.

Leivik. Well, good-night. [*Exit.*]

Isaac. Good-night, Leivik.

Hinde [*from the outer room*]. How is he? Asleep already?

Leivik [*from the outer room*]. Not at all! He's lying on the floor. [Leivik *and* Hinde *appear at the outer door.*]

Hinde. Fie! Get up, Isaac!

LEIVIK. Isaac, hadn't I better. . . . [ISAAC *is silent.* LEIVIK *makes a gesture of despair and leaves.*]

HINDE. Dead drunk. [*Disappears after* LEIVIK. *Both remain talking for a while in the outer room.* HINDE's *laughter is heard, followed by " Good-night!" from* LEIVIK. *The street door is heard being closed. Silence.* HINDE *appears once more at the outer door, looks at* ISAAC, *utters several expressions of disgust and disappears.*— *The room becomes even darker; the glass lamp-chimney has gathered soot. Only a small circle of light about the table is visible, barely revealing the form of* PINYE, *who walks about slowly.*]

PINYE [*soon coming to a stop over* ISAAC]. Dead. Dead.

ISAAC [*sobbing*]. Yes, Death. Death.

PINYE. [*resumes his pacing*]. Dead. Everything. Dark. Cold. Dark and cold. And buried. And decayed. And devoured by worms. And dark. And cold. Cold. Cold. [*Stops and utters strange sounds, sharp, sibilant, like those of a moaning dog.*]

ISAAC [*he has sat up and buried his head in his hands. Suddenly he turns around and stretches himself out on his stomach, with his face to the cupboard*].

BAYLYE [*turning over and talking in her sleep*]. How terribly unhappy I am. Terribly, terribly . . .

PINYE [*ceases moaning and resumes walking about*]. Dark. Dark. Dark. [*Moans as before.*]

ISAAC [*sits up suddenly with a horrible outcry*]. Baylye, I've swallowed the rat-poison! Baylye! Quick! I've swallowed the poison! I didn't want to do it, Baylye, I don't want to die! Baylye, quick!

BAYLYE [*jumping out of bed, terrified*]. What has happened? Good God! What has happened?

Isaac. Baylye, I didn't mean to do it! I didn't mean to! I don't want to. I don't want to . . .

Baylye. What don't you want? Good God, what has happened?

Isaac [*sitting up, his feet stretched out and his head sinking over, his hands in his hair*]. I've swallowed the rat-poison. I didn't want to die. I don't want to die. [Baylye *goes into hysterics.* Pinye *stands over* Isaac, *inquisitively. The children wake up and commence to cry.— There is a sound of opening doors and pattering of bare feet.*]

Isaac [*shrieking*]. I don't want to die! I don't want to—!

CURTAIN

THE LAST JEW

A TRAGEDY IN FOUR ACTS

[1903–4]

AUTHOR'S FOREWORD

This is not a pogrom-tragedy, but the tragedy of a sole survivor, the tragedy of a moribund religion, of a crumbling world-philosophy. Who can say that this is exclusively Jewish?

PERSONS OF THE DRAMA

REB MAYSHE, *the city preacher.*
YEKEF, *his son.*
MINYE, *Yekef's wife.*
LEON ⎫
REUBEN ⎬ *The sons of* YEKEF *and* MINYE.
LIPMAN ⎭
EDA, *granddaughter of Reb Mayshe by another son.*
HERSHMAN, *a banker.*
YOUNG HERSHMAN, *his son.*
THE RABBI.
FIRST DAYON.[1]
SECOND DAYON.
THE STOUT SYNAGOGUE-IDLER.
THE THIN SYNAGOGUE-IDLER.
THE YELLOW JEW.
THE YELLOW JEW'S WIFE.
THE JEW IN THE SOFT HAT.
THE JEW IN THE CAP.
THE YOUNG MAN WHO IS ENGAGED.
THE DUMB BEGGAR-WOMAN.
MEN, WOMEN, AND CHILDREN.

Place: The exile.
Time: A bitter one for Jews.

[1] Assistant to a Rabbi, and well versed in religious law.

ACT I

A spacious room in the Zwie household, neatly furnished. To the right, an oil-cloth couch with a dining-table before it, and chairs about the table. Above the couch hang photographs. To the left, two curtained windows, adorned with flowers. In the foreground, a small table, upon which is placed a candelabra. In the background, the door to the front of the house and to the other rooms. To the right of the door a tile-oven, to the left a glass cupboard, on which lies REB MAYSHE'S *fur-cap.*

It is the last day of Passover. REB MAYSHE, YEKEF, MINYE, LEON, REUBEN *and* LIPMAN *are seated around the table, finishing their meal. Their faces reveal sadness and worry.* LEON, REUBEN *and* LIPMAN *soon arise from their places.* LEON *lights a cigarette and walks over to the forward window.* REUBEN *and* LIPMAN *pace up and down the room, picking their teeth, absorbed in thought.*

REB MAYSHE. Well, we've finished the last Passover meal, praised be the Lord. Ah! . . .

MINYE [*sighing*]. Yes, yes. I could hardly lift a thing to my mouth, and now my hands fairly refuse to make a move toward cleaning off the table.

REB MAYSHE. Dear God, you know my heart. Rather would I have fasted, rather would I have eaten nothing but a doughnut and ashes, if it were not that this holiday is so sacred to you. Look upon my having eaten as a great sacrifice, and ward off from your Holy Scroll and your chosen people a new disaster.

MINYE. Dear God, Lord of the universe!

REB MAYSHE. The last day of Passover! On that day, dear God, I have been wont to rejoice with song and dance; to make merry all day long, to praise and glorify your holy name for the countless favors you have showered upon your chosen people. Most merciful One, for this time, count it enough from us that we have not wept, that we have not moistened our food with our tears, that we have not made of this joyous holiday a day of mourning. [MINYE *bursts into tears.*] Well, let us pray. It is not right to cry, Minye.— Dry your eyes and pray with a devout heart. Pray for yourself and for your sons, and perhaps God will have compassion. [*Begins to pray, emphasizing each word.* MINYE *covers her eyes with her handkerchief and prays quietly.* YEKEF *prays quickly, swaying rapidly to and fro. After they have finished praying, they turn their attention to the conversation of* YEKEF's *three sons.*]

LEON [*as if continuing an interrupted controversy*]. And you'll see, the fright will blow over.

LIPMAN. I hope to God it will! But it's bad enough that talk of another massacre is in the air,— that it is considered a possibility.

LEON [*with weak sarcasm*]. Possibility!

LIPMAN. Be honest, Leon. Don't you feel just like all of us, that there's a pogrom brewing? Can't you see the dark clouds hovering over the Jews, and the menacing insolence that darts from the Christians' eyes?

LEON. Exaggeration! Exaggeration!

LIPMAN. You're beaten, Leon. Burn all those songs

and books of yours. Despite what you've written in them, Life has belied you.

LEON [*at a loss*]. A-hm!

LIPMAN. Your movements were false from beginning to end. Your whole fabric of assimilation was nothing but a soap-bubble. You felt happy, in the Gentile heaven, as a dissenter, as a deserter from the Jews. And now you must arise as a Jew, with a broken head in the bargain.

LEON [*sarcastically*]. Well spoken.

LIPMAN. It'll do you little good to pass all this by with a joke on your lips, while inside your heart is bleeding. Leon, we are strangers, we are in exile. We are powerless, without any rights. In the eyes of all we are insignificant,— we are scorned, despite our capabilities. Our very virtues are made the target of disgrace and mockery. Everywhere we are looked upon as leprous intruders. If we do not willingly remove ourselves, we are thrust aside by force. Wherefore, we must be gone. We must retreat! Retreat! Retreat! We must go home, we must become independent, have a nation of our own, a voice in our own government. We must learn to be ourselves.

REUBEN [*who has been pacing up and down during the foregoing conversation*]. Exactly! Exactly!— I agree to every word you've spoken regarding his beliefs and assimilation. For it's after all not assimilation, but rather a kind of intrusion,— forcing yourself upon a strange people. No good can come of that. You're right there. And it's right, too, that a home, independence, and a nation of our own *would* be a perfect solution to the age-old Jewish problem. But . . . I'll go as far as that " would " with you, and no further. Just explain this to me, will you? For thousands of years the

Jewish people have not ceased to dream of a land of their own. They created a Messiah and flocked after false Messiahs. And more: the Jews to-day, with staff and wallet, stand ready to roam from one land to another, seeking where they may dwell in greatest freedom and security.— How is it, then, that you cannot win the Jews to your cause? How is it that they do not flock to you with all their strength and energy to achieve a nation of their own, and independence? Your ideal should fire all Jewish minds like a spark in a powder magazine. A single call, and every heart that has so long been yearning for deliverance from the bitter exile should turn to you.

LIPMAN. And they *are* turned to me!

REUBEN. Are you in your right senses?

LIPMAN. Yes! Yes! Yes! They *are* turned to me! Every Jewish heart is turned to me. My Zionist movement is a movement of the people.

REUBEN. My dear fellow, that's all mere talk! There's no arguing that point with you. But just consider this: how can the people follow your leadership, when they can't see the road over which they can battle to its goal? For what purpose shall they organize? To do nothing? How is a movement of the people possible when there is no motion? Moses summoned his people to Canaan,— the Promised Land. The way which he pointed out to them lay across a sea and a wilderness, and through armed tribes. The people arose and answered the call. A perilous way, yet at least a way. You go to your people to-day and say, " I have a land for you, but it can be won only by bow and arrow, with musket and powder, and with countless human sacrifices." Then, although I belong to a different camp, I can't deny that you'd attract a great people's movement to your standard and that there would be lively doings in your camp. But as it is . . .

LIPMAN [*interrupting him*]. The fact that I can't come to my people with such a message is the saddest part of my lot. What wouldn't I give if I might do so! Yet the people *are* with me. Our movement is like a great stream that is dammed by boards. Let but the boards be pushed aside, and the waters will rush forth victoriously and inundate the entire country. Wait! The boards will soon be thrust aside.

REUBEN. Fortunate fellow! He paints pictures and consoles himself with them. Don't you know that a people's movement should resemble a powerful stream that tears away all barriers? If it waits until the boards are removed, it may become meanwhile foul and stagnant. And such the Jewish people became behind the boards which its Messiah-faith placed before it. Such will it become behind your Zion-ideal, unless you find at once a way in which the ideal may be fulfilled. Do you know how you can accomplish it? Can you, above all, behold its fulfilment?

LIPMAN. Yes. I behold its fulfilment and I believe in it, and I live it, every day of my life, in every limb and nerve . . .

REUBEN. But those are mere words!

LIPMAN. Enough of your talk and your ridicule. Pray understand me — Often I feel as if I were the embodiment of the millennial hope of the Jews, and I lose myself in longing and give way to tears like a child. Neither you nor he, none of you, in fact, has ever seen me. I clench my fists, stretch out my arms and plant myself squarely upon my feet and cry out: "Independence! Independence! Independence!" In my dreams I behold our own land as clear as reality,— and the foreign earth upon which I tread burns my feet. Not only here, under the oppression of hatred and massacres, do I feel that I tread on foreign soil and that my feet burn from the contact. It is the same amidst the greatest freedom and equality, under the most friendly and fraternal conditions. Even the most just equality is not independence, and independence alone can be the reward of our people for its centuries of suffering. Ah! That is my deepest yearning, and my mission is to make my people see what I see, to experience what I experience, to feel what I feel, and to will what I will. The man in us Jews must be aroused, so that we shall no longer be content to be slaves; and once we have become men, the Jew in us must be revived, and the independence of our people be dearer to us than anything else in the world. This is my work; in this work lies the guarantee that the water will not become a swamp before the boards are removed. Laugh if you will, but all this is so!

REUBEN. You're wrong; I'll not laugh at you. Rather shall I pity you. You're wandering, brother, and you'll lead nowhere. Before you know it, we'll turn your stream from behind your boards into the deep, wide ocean of people's freedom and international brotherhood. And the reward of the Jewish people for its centuries of suffering,— if you *must* have a reward! — will be the most significant, even the foremost position in the battle of humanity for its liberation. That, in my eyes, is the greatest reward and the most ideal historic justice. Yes, brother, our way lies open and the masses that enter upon it grow continually greater. Our cause gains strength from day to day. Nothing can oppose our growth. We triumph over the greatest obstacles. We grow with the rapidity of a snowball that rolls down a snowy mountain, and woe to him who gets in our way. I tell you, Socialism will . . .

YEKEF [*springing to his feet*]. Tfu! May its name and its memory be obliterated! I believe I've told you before that you are not to mention that word under my roof. It's the root of all our sorrows. If only Jewish children had nothing to do with it, we'd know nothing of curses and massacres. And take my word for it, some day all of us will get after you and wipe you out so completely that not a trace will be left.

REUBEN. Do you know, father, that if a massacre were not in itself a contemptible thing, I'd say that you had fully earned it. And if you weren't my father . . .

YEKEF [*with more heat*]. If I weren't your father you'd be rotting at the bottom of hell by now. And I warn you to take care hereafter, for your being my son won't stand in my way. . . . [*Greatly excited.*] And an end to all this, I say! An end!

REUBEN. Between us all was at an end long ago. And don't get so excited for nothing. There are bigger and stronger people than you, and we're not afraid of them, either.

YEKEF. I'll show you, I'll teach you. . . .

MINYE. What's the use of all this quarreling? [*To* REUBEN.] Don't mind what he says.— Now I say differently: Let's agree that all of these ideas are good, just, practicable,— that Lipman will lead us in peace to the Holy Land and rebuild our Temple, and that Reuben will bring down a heaven upon earth. That's all very nice. But until then? Until then they'll kill us out so that not one of us will be left. What use to me is all this talk about to-morrow? How about now? — the present?

Lipman [*impatient*]. The present! . . . The present . . . !

Reuben. The present, mother dear? The present is not very hopeful.

Reb Mayshe [*who has heard all this while leaning against the tile-oven*]. There they stand, the wise men, the enlightened ones, the educated leaders, who have dethroned God and want to run the world themselves.— There they stand with open mouths, full of tongue, and are at a loss to reply to a simple word like "the present." And not to answer is to them an answer, too! Answer! Else to the devil with you, or come back to God!

Lipman. But, grandpa, the question isn't a question, either. For thousands of years the Jews have suffered and have borne the most grievous sorrows with iron patience. That same patience must not desert us before the happy end arrives.

Reb Mayshe. Yes. For thousands of years our strength came from our God, and our patience from our faith. But you would accomplish everything with human hands alone, without God and against our faith. That's why to-day we have neither strength nor patience.

Lipman. Those are mere words that unreasonable people insist upon using. And I tell you, grandpa, we are a dispersed people, a haphazard people. Didn't Moses reproach us with the same charge, and doesn't the Talmud judge us likewise? A people that refuses to recognize that a nation is not built in a night,— nor a people established in a day. We can suffer in silence for eternities, but no sooner are we shown a way out than we lose all patience. And instead of setting quietly to work, we disturb matters with our impatience and our questions about "the present."

Reb Mayshe. And I tell you that you're nothing but apostates and blasphemers. You mention Moses and the Talmud only to blaspheme both. That's what I say. You bring contamination, not help. You are destroyers, not builders. You are blind, I say. Blind! You are groping in the darkness and think you see a way out. What do you know of straight or crooked, right or wrong? How do you know what to-morrow can bring forth? What do you know of the secrets behind the motion of God's world? You plan, but you trace your plans upon sands that the smallest breeze may blow away. You build, but your structures are like Jonah's gourd that sprang up during the night and vanished as quickly. Your vanity proposes, and God disposes. What proof can you advance that this is not so? And how can you assume such a responsibility before your people, who will fall into a deeper abyss of dejection when it learns that it has been not led, but led astray? Oh, you ridiculous clowns! I tell you, our strength is in God, and our patience is in our faith. We know that God is punishing us,— that God sends us our sorrows, and we welcome them gladly because we know too, that He is a merciful Father, and that He will put an end to our trials and establish us again. Nor do we ask about the present. Like a rock in the midst of a stormy sea, smitten by wind and tempest and mountain-like waves,— even so firm do we stand. The forces of the storm loosen and break off countless bits of the rock, but it stands fast and high as ever. It laughs its enemies to scorn, and knows that sooner or later the sun will burst through the clouds and dry it, warming and cheering it with its beams. Even so is the chosen people, when it is strong in its faith and holds fast to the Holy Law. That is why I always cry with the prophet:

"Return, ye backsliding children!" Return, ye who have strayed, and embraced false teachings! Return, ye who have led the people astray, and ye who have followed the false leaders! Return to God and His law! Be steadfast to your faith! There shall come a redeemer to Zion!

MINYE. Amen! Lord of the universe!

LEON. Grandpa, I've never seen you so beautiful before. I looked at you as you spoke and it seemed I was living through a poem.

REB MAYSHE [*eyes him for a moment, with scorn*]. Tfu! You deaf ears,— you callous hearts!

REUBEN. True, grandpa. We can enjoy you only with our eyes. But not with our ears or our hearts. What you were just now preaching, grandpa, is darkness itself.

REB MAYSHE. Aha! Darkness, fanaticism! . . . Ah! Why do I waste time talking to you? It is our strength and our life, our patience and our support in all the long, bitter exile; and here they come — the clowns — and call it darkness and heaven knows what else!

REUBEN. Yes, darkness, brought down from the dark ages, when darkness lay upon all the peoples. And no matter how much or how poetically you speak, your voice will not be heard. Grandpa, I'm sorry for you — your day has vanished into the past. You were born too late. Your sermons will turn no one back, even if you should weep the bitterest of tears. And this is so not because we, the younger generation, the new preachers, are against you and talk the people away from you, but because life itself is against you. Life, almighty life, has taken the people away from you forever and ever. We, the new preachers, merely provide the people with new ideas, new thoughts, and a new faith,— with new heavens and a new law.

REB MAYSHE. Woe to the ears that must hear such words!

REUBEN. There's no help for it, and I'm sorry for you, grandpa. You stand all alone,— the last Jew, the solitary survivor of a departed day. The world belongs to us, to me . . .

REB MAYSHE. You lie! I am not a sole survivor, neither do I stand all alone. The world does not belong to you, nor shall it belong to you. Our true God still lives and will be victorious over all your idols. Remember, " Israel is not a widower." Israel has plenty of pious Jews, and will have enough in the future. God of Abraham! If I ever knew that I was the sole remaining pious Jew, I should long ago have prayed God to take me away from this world of sin. But it is not so. And I'll live to see the day when all of you will come back to the bosom of our Law, when you'll all repent, and weep and wail over your errors. Yes, I'll live to see that day. I know I shall. God will lengthen my years, if need be.— Oh, great, powerful, omnipotent God, reveal your power, reveal it. Prove that you still live . . . [*From the street come sounds of running about. There is a noise of doors and shutters being closed.*]

MINYE. Oh, Good Lord, what can that be? What's the matter? [*She runs out.* REUBEN, LIPMAN *and* LEON *look out through the window.* YEKEF *sinks into a chair.*]

REB MAYSHE [*as if in prayer*]. Now is your time, Father in heaven, now is your time!

YEKEF. I'm trembling all over, upon my word. [*The shutters of the window are closed from the outside. The room becomes half-dark; the light enters only through the shutter-spaces and the door.*]

MINYE [*running in*]. Woe is us! It's begun already, on Broad Street . . .

YEKEF. On Broad Street! Good God! Our store! Our store!

MINYE. . . . And by the river. They drowned two Jews.

YEKEF. On Broad Street! . . . Good God! Our store! [*From the street comes the sound of whistling,— a prearranged signal.* REUBEN *and* LIPMAN *rush to the door.*]

MINYE [*on the threshold*]. What's this? Where are you running to?

REUBEN. You surely know. To our organizations for self-defense.

MINYE. Children, my sons, you shan't leave this house! I'll not let you! You'll have to pass over my body!

YEKEF. Better let us all run to our store! Good heavens! Our store! Let's run to it!

MINYE. What are you talking about, you lunatic! His store! His store!— Children, you shan't leave! My sons, you remain here! You stay here with your mother!

LIPMAN. Don't detain us, mother. We're late as it is. Every minute that we lose is a crime against the community.

YEKEF. Community! There's words for you! Community! Three grown-up sons, and not a bit of use do I get from them! All they think of is the community! Woe to us! We'll have to go a-begging from door to door.

REUBEN [*trying to force his way through the door*]. Mother!

MINYE. You sha'n't leave, children, unless you want me to die! With my ill-health I'll never survive it. I'll go crazy! Children, have pity! If we are destined to be killed, then let us at least die together. Yes, together. My sons, don't go! Every moment I'll imagine that you've already been murdered, that you're sprawling somewhere, bruised and trampled. . . . Oh, God in heaven, God in heaven!

REUBEN. It's no use, mother. Let me pass.

MINYE. Is it nothing to you that your mother will go mad with terror? That she'll die from uncertainty of your fate?

LIPMAN. Mother, brace up and be brave. If you were a true Jewish mother, you would not hold us back, but rather send us forth. You should be proud, you should rejoice that we go with such willingness. Let us pass, mother. Be strong, have courage and know that if we cannot live like men, let us at least die like men!

MINYE [*breaks into wailing and leaves a free passage for her sons.* REUBEN *and* LIPMAN *hurry out*].

YEKEF [*calling after them*]. Children! Heartless wretches!

MINYE [*sobbing*]. Woe is me! Woe is me!

REUBEN [*at the door*]. If you're afraid to remain here, I can tell you a good hiding-place. In the big forest, about five hundred paces from Hershel the blacksmith's place, you'll come to the forest-warden's house. Tell him I sent you. He'll hide you well. A good many cowardly Jews will probably join you. There you can sit in safety and scare yourselves to your hearts' content. [*Disappears.*]

YEKEF. Heartless wretches they are! Not children! Woe! Woe! We'll become beggars. Beggars!

MINYE. Dear God! Let them at least return to me alive!

REB MAYSHE [*takes the fur-cap from the cupboard, and puts it on over his skull-cap*]. Well, now I go, too.

MINYE. Where? What?

REB MAYSHE. To *my* organization.

YEKEF. What's this? What's this? Upon my word, he's crazy!

REB MAYSHE. You don't know my organization, then? Remarkable! — [*Cuttingly.*] I'm going to the synagogue. That is my organization. The synagogue and the Holy Scrolls of the Law must be defended.

YEKEF. And he's the defender!

REB MAYSHE. Then come! *You* be the defender.

MINYE. What are you talking about, father? Is this for your years and your strength?

REB MAYSHE. You are younger and stronger. Come along.

MINYE. Yes! Just you and I. Little it'll take to finish us. One blow and we're done for.

REB MAYSHE. Spare your talk, woman. You'll not hold me back. I learned a lesson from your sons who just left. O, Jews, Jews! If we cannot live like Jews, let us at least die like Jews! To the synagogue! You should not restrain me. No, you should come with me! You should not run to your place of hiding, but should go to the synagogue and stand up for your holy possessions, lest they be soiled by unclean hands.— Out of my way, or I'll curse you! [MINYE, *crushed, yields.*]

LEON. Grandpa, I'm afraid you'll be the only one in the synagogue, and when they attack it, you'll not be able to defend the Holy Scrolls, and will succeed only in bringing death upon yourself.

Reb Mayshe. I'll be the only one there, you say? Ha-ha! I am the sole survivor, the last one. Ha-ha! — I'll be the only one? No, no! Only I shall feel a deep shame that not one of my children will be there.

Leon. I hope you are right, and that you will not be alone. Then your life will be in less danger.

Reb Mayshe. Never mind your good wishes. Better come along with me now.

Leon. Stay here, and I'll risk my life. . . .

Reb Mayshe. No more words! Even if you had come with me I should have slammed the door in your face and locked you out. You want to protect me, not the Holy Scroll. You would be a hindrance to God's army, — a desecration. Stay behind, where you're known! Hide in the woods and tremble with the other cowards. You have earned your fright most honorably. [*About to leave.*]

Minye. Father-in-law! Oh, father!

Yekef. Did you ever see? They've all got their petty interests. . . .

Reb Mayshe. Be silent, lest I thank God in my last moments that not you will close my eyes — O, sinners, sinners! Little do you realize what a day this may turn out to be! To us it is the last day of a holy week, yet it may be a first day to God. God's faithful will become martyrs, and soon strayed children will turn back to their Father, callous hearts will again throb with Judaism, and the weak and faltering will once more find strength in their Lord.— To-day is your time, O God; to-day is your time! [*He leaves.*]

Minye [*breaking into tears anew*]. What a day, good Lord, what a day! O, that I had not lived to see it!

LEON [*as if to himself*]. A day of great reckoning.

YEKEF. They've all got their petty interests, and when it comes to the important thing there's nobody at hand.— Woe is me, what's to be done? What can we begin to do? [*Looks at* LEON.] Good Lord, our store! We'll be left paupers! What's to be done? What's to be done?

LEON [*bluntly*]. Do you want an answer from me?

YEKEF. By all means. Suggest something. Speak!

LEON. Rush to your store and defend it. Take a stick or a broom, or an old osier brush and protect your precious store, your holy realm, your soul.

YEKEF. What! You're poking fun at me! Ridicule! Here I am weeping tears of blood, and all you can do is poke fun at me!

LEON. I am in dead earnest. If your store is more to you than anything else . . .

YEKEF. Enough of your joking, I tell you. Do you hear? You'll see how we'll get along without the store. And then you'll know whether it's a joke or not!

LEON. No. I'm not poking fun at you, but only at myself. I'm ridiculing myself alone. How blind I've been! With you always before my eyes I never noticed grandpa and my brothers. With you always before my eyes, you assumed the stature of the whole Jewish people, and I was disgusted with it.

YEKEF. What do you want, eh? Why have you set upon me now? Am I not suffering enough without your adding to it?

LEON. What do I want, eh? I want to confess; I want to speak my mind, to pour out my wrath. . . .

YEKEF. Well, what do you think of this! You want to pour out your wrath on me, perhaps?

LEON. On you, yes! On you! Because through you

I conceived a disgust for the whole Jewish race. It looked to me as petty as yourself,— a horde of petty money-grabbers,— without a heart, without a soul, without a will or an impulse to something higher,— without the strength to live or the courage to die. And I despised it from the bottom of my heart! I tried to stifle within me every remembrance that I was a Jew. Everything in me that came from the Jews, from you, I strove to root out of my nature,— to forget, to destroy. I wanted to free myself of you, of myself. . . .

YEKEF [*who has not been listening to him*]. Enough! My learned professor! Just as if he had an audience. Breaks out into a sermon!

LEON [*eyeing him with a scorn*]. Oh, you. . . . Unhappy soul!

MINYE [*in tears*]. What a day, Lord of the universe, what a day!

YEKEF. What's to be done? I can't imagine. My head is splitting. . . . And what are we sitting here for? Are we waiting for them to come to us?

MINYE. Let them come. Let them smash the place to bits; let them kill everybody. It's all the same to me now.

YEKEF. You're just as crazy as your sons! Perhaps you, too, want to confess and pour out your heart.

MINYE. Oh, I confessed and poured out my heart long ago. During all my life with you, and afterwards bringing up the children, not a day went by that I didn't pour out my heart. But I did it within me, because I wanted nobody to hear. Besides there was nobody to talk to. But the Lord heard. He was with me everywhere,— in the kitchen, in the dining-room, in the store. He knows my heart; I need no more.

YEKEF. Enough from you, my pious one. And let's

be off to the hiding-place that Reuben spoke of. We've got to take your jewelry along, and the silverware. We'll lock the house and leave. If our home isn't attacked, then certainly all thanks to the Lord; if it is, let us at least save ourselves and the little gold and silver that we own.

MINYE [*sarcastically*]. Excellent!

YEKEF. Then move,— get up. Do something!

MINYE [*rises with an effort. A knocking at the door*].

YEKEF [*in a frightened voice*]. Hush! I think somebody's knocking at the door. [*The knocking grows louder.*]

EDA [*from without*]. Open the door. It's I, Eda.

MINYE. Eda? [*Goes out.*]

LEON [*about to rush to the other part of the house, but stops on the threshold of the doorway*].

YEKEF. Eda? A fine time to choose for a visit, upon my word!

MINYE [*comes in with* EDA, *who is in the costume of a red-cross nurse, with a black cross hanging from her neck*].

EDA [*giving* LEON *her hand, and holding him thus during the ensuing conversation*]. I'm glad to find you here, Leon dear.— How dark it is!— I can make out Uncle. But where's grandpa? Where's Reuben? And Lipman?

MINYE [*tearfully*]. They have all gone. Reuben and Lipman have *their* organizations, and your grandpa has *his,*— the synagogue.

YEKEF. What's doing anyway? Tell us. Say something. Were you, perhaps, on Broad Street?

EDA. Who can go through Broad Street now?

YEKEF. Oh, woe is me! Oh, woe is me!

EDA. It's already spread to the riverfront, and the side streets and Long Street. If it weren't for my redcross uniform, I could never have reached you.

YEKEF. Oh! Minye! Do you hear? Minye! Hurry! What are you standing there for? Move! Do something!

MINYE [*angered*]. Move yourself! Do something yourself! What are you ordering me about for? [*Begins to collect the spoons and forks from the table.*]

YEKEF [*stumbling over a chair*]. Oh, my feet give way under me, upon my word.

EDA. What are you going to do? Have you a place to go to?

MINYE. How should I know? Reuben told us of a hiding-place. As if any one can hide from God. There's no hiding from Him. His thunder can strike anywhere.— Ah!— And your folks? Where are they?

EDA [*laughs in embarrassment*].

MINYE [*surprised*]. Well? What is it?

EDA. Would that all the Jews were as safe as they. [LEON *looks at her sharply.* EDA *nods to him and points to her cross.*] A-hm!

LEON [*gasping*]. Impossible!

MINYE [*dropping her silverware upon the table and hastening over to* EDA]. Eda dear, I don't understand deaf-and-dumb language. What has happened to you and your folks?

EDA. An acquaintance of ours . . . a Christian, took us into his home.

MINYE [*somewhat incredulous*]. A Christian acquaintance?

YEKEF. Minye! Minye! This is no time for conversations. Where are the keys? Have you got them?

[*Thrusts* MINYE *through the door and goes out with her.*]

LEON [*quickly, in a subdued voice*]. How could you do it?

EDA. What do you mean, " How "?

LEON. Impossible! Impossible!

EDA. And you can talk like that? I can't understand you. We went to the limit of your teaching. You preach assimilation, don't you? Well, what better assimilation than to adopt Christianity altogether?

LEON. We can't go to the limit. We can't adopt Christianity because we don't believe in it. Such adoption is not assimilation. It's hypocrisy.

EDA. Does every believer in assimilation really think that he's ceased to be a Jew? Isn't he really something of a hypocrite? No, Leon, my father is right. To go only half way is nonsense. We're unbelievers anyway, and exchange a bad form of unbelief for a good one,— a peaceful one. And it's not at all impossible that our children should grow up into sincere Christians. The step had to be taken.— I really can't understand you.

LEON. Eda, our ways have parted. Far, very far from each other. We are at opposite poles. I am not to-day the same Leon Zwie I was yesterday.

EDA. Speak more clearly. Don't frighten me, Leon dear!

LEON. Which is the greater and the more honorable, Eda,— self-humiliation or self-liberation? Self-denial or self-assertion? I trod the path of self-humiliation and self-denial, while about me were Jews who went the way of self-liberation and self-assertion,— Jews full of strength, of life, of power, Jews of indomitable will and gigantic faith. . . .

EDA. Who? Your father, perhaps?

LEON. Don't mock, Eda. Don't let my petty father hide from your sight my noble grandfather and my noble brothers.

EDA. What's come over you? I can't understand you any more!

LEON. Oh, if you had but gone through what I am going through to-day!

EDA [*puts her arm around his neck and caresses him*]. Come to yourself, Leon dear. You'll travel the same road as I.

LEON. Impossible forever! I'll never take the step you have taken. And to-day I am further from it than ever.

EDA. Leon, what are you saying? How can you speak like that? In the name of our love, Leon . . .

LEON. You will have to turn back.

EDA. Under no circumstances! That would be madness!

LEON. Eda, even in the gloom of our room I can see that the costume of a red-cross nurse becomes you very much. It is a long time since I have beheld you looking so beautiful. The semi-darkness embraces your white form so secretly, and lends a mystic charm to your face. If I had not loved you before, I should have fallen in love with you now. . . .

EDA. Don't speak sweet words to me at such a moment.

LEON. I'll not speak sweet words, but bitter ones. I want to tell you that with all my great love for you, I'll not take the step you have taken. I'm standing now at a parting of ways, but I'll not choose the road you have chosen.— Eda, I have been a slave, with servile thoughts. I was the weakest, and thought myself the strongest. Because Jews are scorned, I erected a theory that we are not ourselves, that we must not be ourselves. Because Jews are ridiculed, I saw in them only the petty individuals and the petty characteristics, — all that was low and vulgar. Everything Jewish was evil to my eyes,— worse than to the eyes of the Gentiles. I fawned upon the Gentiles, I humiliated myself and raised self-humiliation aloft as a banner, as the highest goal of our ambition. Eda, we have sinned against the Jews,— have insulted and destroyed the free man within us! . . .

EDA. Bah! Reactionary talk! Mere reaction! Who talked you into all this? Your grandpa, the fanatic preacher? Or Lipman, the Utopian? Or was it Reuben, the Socialist Jew who's going to turn the world upside down? Did your whole doctrine stand on such straw-legs? Did the pogrom surprise you so much? — Leon! Leon!

MINYE [*enters as* EDA *utters the last sentence*]. Eda, I can't get it out of my head. There's something wrong about your family's connection with that Christian acquaintance. You laughed so queerly when you mentioned it. [*Looks at* EDA *piercingly, and utters her words with slow emphasis.*] Tell me the truth.

EDA [*resolutely*]. Yes, I will. Father, mother,— all of us have become Christians.

MINYE [*clutching her bosom, then her head*]. Oh! Oh! Oh! [*She is about to fall.* LEON *catches her.*]

YEKEF [*comes running in with various bundles under his arms and in his hands*]. What's the matter? What's the matter?

MINYE [*in a choking voice*]. They have become Christians. Oh! Oh! Oh!

YEKEF. Christians? Woe is me! Woe is me! [*The bundles fall from his grasp.*]

EDA [*in a conciliating tone*]. You know how it is. We were never very pious Jews anyway. Then why should we suffer from massacres? Really. Since we were already practically Gentiles, why shouldn't we become real Gentiles and stop suffering Jewish sorrows? Now, at least, we are safe from harm. The priest is in our home and . . .

YEKEF. Oh! Woe is me! Woe is me!

MINYE. Then why did you come here? To boast of your priest and your security? To increase our sorrows? To grieve us to death? Thank God that grandfather went away! He would have fallen dead where he stood; he could have never survived the news. Whatever death he may die to-day, the most cruel, the most horrible death will be sweeter than that he would have died here. Oh! Oh! Oh! [*In a rage.*] Out! Out of my home! Out, I say! Out! [*Becomes hysterical.*]

YEKEF. Yes! Out! Out with you! [*Aided by* LEON *he places* MINYE *upon the couch. They open her waist and pour down her throat a restorative, which* LEON *has brought from the cupboard.* EDA, *at a loss, goes to the door.* MINYE *gradually calms down, and sobs quietly.*]

EDA [*softly*]. Leon.

LEON [*motioning to her*]. Better leave now. [EDA *looks at him for a moment. Her face twitches with inner pain. She leaves.* MINYE's *sobbing subsides.*]

YEKEF [*beginning to pick up his bundles. There is a far-off noise of many voices. From the street the sound of running to and fro*]. Oh! Oh! I'm afraid that . . . I'll die of fright, upon my word. . . . Oh! They've reached our street already. Minye! Minye! What shall we do? [MINYE *sits up.*]

LEON. We'll stay right here. Where can we go now, with her in such a condition?

MINYE. Has she gone?

LEON. Yes, mother.

MINYE. And you? You don't follow her? You won't become a . . . ?

LEON. No, mother.

MINYE [*caresses his head and kisses him*]. Then I'm well again. Now I can go as far as you wish.— You, Yekef, take your bundles. I'll take my son.

YEKEF [*taking the bundles*]. Oh! Woe is me! Oh! Woe is me! If we can only dodge through the streets in safety. I'll have to hide the bundles somewhere in the yard. Oh! Woe is me! [*They leave,* MINYE *leaning against* LEON.]

CURTAIN

ACT II

FIRST SCENE

Interior of the synagogue. In the center, the pulpit, with steps leading to it in front and from the rear. About it are grouped benches, before which stand several lecterns. To the left, the Holy Ark, on a high platform; underneath, the altar, upon which is placed a large silver seven-branched candlestick in which candles are burning. The altar is covered with an old, threadbare, velvet tablecloth; the Holy Ark is hung with a curtain on which is embroidered in gold thread a David's Shield (six-pointed star), and a short top-curtain, upon which are embroidered in gold and silver thread, and spangles, two lions, holding a small David's Shield. On each side of the Holy Ark are rows of brightly painted benches, with high backs and book-rests in front of them. On each side of the room, two large windows. At the rear, three high windows; along the wall, benches without backs. Before the benches, long tables. Not far from the right stands a tall grandfather's clock. The entrance door is to the right. On each side of the door, a high tile oven. Above, the windows of the women's section.

Two synagogue idlers, one of them tall and stout, the other short and thin, are discovered sitting on the pulpit-bench, near the Holy Ark, their book-rests

before them. *On the latter lie large volumes of the
Gemara. The idlers are swaying before their
books, humming the chanting-tunes to which the
Gemara is read, but not pronouncing any words.
Both are about thirty years of age, and very poorly
clad.*

The Thin One [*with the chanting intonation*]. Do you know what I'll tell you? I'm as hungry as a bear.

The Stout One [*the same*]. And if *you* are hungry, then what shall *I* say? If you are hungry once, then I am hungry seventy-seven fold.

The Thin One. A fine last day of Passover! I tell you!

The Stout One [*still chanting*]. Just what I'm insisting upon!

The Thin One. I know I'm not much of an eater. In fact, sometimes a dry crumb is enough for me from one Sabbath to another. But to fast on such a day as this . . . !

The Stout One. Could anything be worse than my case? I always used to eat so much on the last day of Passover that even I, you'll understand, even I, couldn't eat for a week and had an awful pressure against my sides! First of all, I used to accompany my host on his round of visits. And his list of relatives,— may no evil eye gaze upon them,— was a long one, indeed. For he's Mr. Shlayme Peshelis, I'll have you know! And wherever we went they feasted us royally. May every son of Israel be as well off as each of Shlayme's relatives! — And you may just bet that in those days I certainly ate my fill! That was what you call eating! Why should I be stingy with their food? So down it went! I let nothing go by. And after that, late in the afternoon, when we'd come home, the real feast began, you'll understand. The real feast began. We'd eat and drink till sunset prayers, you'll understand.— We'd say sunset prayers, then go back to our feast, and the same with evening prayers — and we'd eat away, you'll understand, till long after dark, and then return to leavened bread in the shape of a nice, fresh, hot roll. . . .

THE THIN ONE [*groaning*]. What's the use of talking? To-day they were all in such a hurry. . . .

THE STOUT ONE. To-day? Don't mention it! As to visiting, it was not to be thought of. People were afraid to show themselves upon the street. And they ate with such haste that the haste of the Jews in Egypt, which we commemorate with our unleavened bread, was slowness itself aside of it. First of all, there was nothing to eat that required the use of spoons, because the spoons are of silver and they were afraid that somebody might steal them from before their very eyes. Devil take such folks, say I! Better have wooden spoons and hand me a plate of fine soup,— a borshtch — with an aroma that goes through every bone in your body. And some meat that's been cooked with it, that'll . . . you understand . . . Isn't it so? . . . eh?

THE THIN ONE [*his mouth watering*]. Oy, oy! . . . Do you really think there's going to be a massacre?

THE STOUT ONE. And if there *is* a pogrom, what then? Mustn't we eat in the meantime? I stick to my motto. Wait. Take your time! You must always take it for granted that there will be no pogrom. The Jews inhabit six hundred and eighty cities and towns, and in each one of them they talk of massacres. Can there be a massacre in every one of these six hundred and eighty places? Ridiculous, say I! Then why should I imagine that the pogrom will strike my particular town?

People are talking about it, you say? But they're talking about it everywhere! Rather let us imagine that there won't be any massacre at all, and let's be reasonable creatures — not spoil such a fine holiday as this, you'll understand. Such a last day of Passover. But a massacre is likely to happen after all, you say? Then there's always time to hide oneself, isn't there? Hey?

The Thin One. As far as I'm concerned, you're right. I can easily find a place to hide in. But take, for example, a fellow like yourself?

The Stout One. I have such an excellent place to hide in, that if I were as well fed as usual on the last day of Passover I could lie there as long as I pleased without the slightest danger of being discovered.

The Thin One. And where might that be?

The Stout One. Right here, underneath the synagogue, you'll understand.

The Thin One. What? Where the pigs congregate?

The Stout One. What of it? I won't eat them, will I?

The Thin One. Well, but . . .

The Stout One. And then again, the pigs could be driven away. Of course, I would beg their pardon very politely, and I'd have more room, too, you'll understand.

The Thin One. For a good many more Jews.

The Stout One. [*with a pious, Gemara intonation*]. And for Jewesses, too!

The Thin One [*beginning once more to sway to and fro, looking into his book and speaking with the pious sing-song*]. And now, where have we reached?

The Stout One [*with sing-song manner*]. We've reached . . . we've reached . . . an agreement that it wouldn't be a bad idea to have a bite.

REB MAYSHE [*enters. He wears his fur-cap and his long coat. He kisses the mazuzah*]. Holy congregation, pardon me if I . . . [*Stops suddenly.*] The synagogue is empty? The — synagogue — empty? [*The idlers sway more piously than ever, and chant very loudly.* REB MAYSHE's *voice changes to one of pleasure.*] No, I was mistaken. Here sit some Jews studying the Holy Law. Thanks, O God, that I have been permitted to hear this. Your children are being persecuted, yet they sit and study the Law. [*He comes forward and sees the idlers. The pleasure vanishes from his features.*] How! Only they! — God, how great is your people of Israel! Its worst members become its best.

THE STOUT ONE. Good holiday to you, Reb Mayshe! Was that you talking?

REB MAYSHE. Good holiday to you, my children, and thanks, too! I was about to open my mouth to utter a curse, when I heard your voices chanting the Holy Law, and my curse was transformed into a blessing.

THE THIN ONE. And whom did you wish to curse?

REB MAYSHE. Whom? The cowards, the weaklings, those who have forgotten God, those who think only of themselves, not of the synagogue. [*Sits down wearily.*] I ran all the way and expected to find a synagogue full of Jews. Listen, children, I ran to the synagogue and told myself that I'd find a full congregation. I beheld young, and old, men, women, and children. My heart melted with joy, and I was at once glad and ashamed that I should be the last to arrive, and I wanted to beg their pardon . . . holy congregation. . . .

THE STOUT ONE. So should it have been, indeed!

REB MAYSHE. Not so? And I enter the synagogue, and am about to speak, when I see that which makes me doubt my eyes — not a Jew present! A horrible thought assailed me and a curse rushed to my tongue, — a curse not written in the Holy Law, but you two took the curse from my mouth. May God's blessing descend upon you and may He refresh you as you have refreshed me. [*Arises, and speaks louder.*] Oh, Israel is not a widower! Israel is not a widower! If only those grandsons of mine, the infidels, could see you here now, how they would blush for shame! What does their courage amount to beside yours? What is their might, what is all their heroism and struggle, compared to your sitting here studying the Law in such a day as this? [*The idlers look at each other slyly and shrug their shoulders.*] But I tell you, children, you must show that your strength is not alone for studying the Law, but to protect it. Even as a stag runs to slake its thirst in a stream, so should we Jews run to study the Torah; but when it comes to defending our sacred possessions against a desecrating hand we should be like lions! We must fear no enemy, however great he be. For, can there be a sweeter death than to die for our scrolls and for His Holy Name? . . . But why should I disturb your study with my talk? Study, my children, study. I'll make all the preparations myself. I know where our caretaker's implements are hidden. You will be brave. You will be brave. [*Hastens through the door.*]

THE STOUT ONE. Do you understand what he's talking about?

THE THIN ONE. And why shouldn't I understand?

THE STOUT ONE. He means,— and I hope the hour will never come — that if the synagogue is attacked, we are to be the defenders and protect the scrolls with our lives.

THE THIN ONE. Oy! Oy! That's asking a great

deal,— to sacrifice one's life for the Lord. Not a trifle, hey?

THE STOUT ONE. Now, tell the truth, could you do it?

THE THIN ONE. I say ... I believe ... I'll tell you the truth. I'd die of fright before they reached anywhere near the synagogue.

THE STOUT ONE. And I'll be in hiding underneath, with the pigs,— so scared that I won't even know how I got there.

THE THIN ONE. Oy! Oy!

THE STOUT ONE. And I've got another splendid idea. The weapons — the axes and the saws and other things — can come in handy down below! For if they should try to crawl in after us, we can give them a slash over the snout with the ax so that the sparks will fly. It's a good thing he reminded us of the weapons.

THE THIN ONE. But something else is on my mind. Suppose they set fire to the synagogue, with us lying underneath it?

THE STOUT ONE. Pessimist! You've got to look at everything from the dark side! In the first place, why should I imagine that they'll set fire to the place? And in the second, the weapons will prove all the more useful to us in such a case.

REB MAYSHE [*enters. Under his right arm he carries an ax; under the left a saw and a pick; with both hands he drags a heavy crowbar. He has great difficulty in closing the door. At sight of him, the idlers resume their pious chanting.* REB MAYSHE, *with much effort, drags himself up to the Holy Ark*]. These, children, are our weapons, and God will strengthen our hands. I'll take the ax. [*Lifts up the ax.*] Ah, it is light enough for my feeble hands, and with it I'll hew down the enemies of the Lord.— You, you big fellow, take the crowbar. It is heavy but in your hand it will be as light as a switch with which to slay the desecrators, just as Samson slew the Philistines.— And you, short and thin as you are, have your choice of the saw or the pick, and whichever you choose, let it become a dangerous weapon in your hands. [*Sighs.*] One of the weapons will remain without arms to wield it. Too bad. God, how small your army is! Only we three,— and I imagined I'd find a full synagogue.— Lord, where are your Jews? Where is your army? Or can three be enough for you? [*Passes his hand over his face and his beard.*] It is wrong to think like this! It is wrong to think in this fashion! No, Israel is not a widower; Israel stands not alone!— Ah, children, you two are already much indeed! And if you two could raise yourselves to such a high degree, why should I think ill of other Jews? They shall yet come! Those who live on the other side of Long Street cannot come, because the rioters are in the way. And those who . . .

THE STOUT ONE. What rioters? Has the massacre started already?

REB MAYSHE [*slowly*]. Then you did not know it until just now?

THE STOUT ONE. I thought the whole thing would blow over without a pogrom. [THE THIN ONE *looks with fright towards the door and the windows, and his teeth begin to chatter.*]

REB MAYSHE. Well! Why have you turned pale all of a sudden, and what have your teeth begun to chatter for? Be firm, soldiers of the Lord! Step up here. Here before the Holy Ark we'll take our stand, unconquerable, yielding to none. . . . [*Both idlers look with fright toward the door and the windows, and neither hears a word that* REB MAYSHE *speaks.*] Be firm, children. Be firm and summon all your courage.

THE STOUT ONE. Have they already reached Long Street? Where did it begin? When did it begin?

REB MAYSHE. What's the difference to you, when or where? The enemy is near; it may burst upon us at any moment. Be firm and ready for them.

THE STOUT ONE. I'll tell you the truth. I still hope to God they won't be able to come to the synagogue street. . . .

THE THIN ONE. Amen, amen! Lord of the universe! Would that they perish miserably before reaching the synagogue street!

REB MAYSHE [*with a penetrating glance at both of them*]. And suppose that, despite all, they invade the synagogue street? [*The idlers look at each other in embarrassment and then cast frightened glances toward the entrance and the windows.* REB MAYSHE *raises his voice.*] Shall you run away? Shall you desert the synagogue and its sacred scrolls?

THE STOUT ONE. But I'm telling you, I hope to God . . .

REB MAYSHE. Silence! Take not His name in vain. [*More calmly.*] Answer me, will you run away? Will you hide yourselves?

THE STOUT ONE. Say yourself, Reb Mayshe, how can we resist the Christians? What can we do against them? We, feeble Jews, bench-warmers? . . .

THE THIN ONE. And mighty hungry ones, moreover.

THE STOUT ONE. Hungry indeed! We've eaten practically nothing to-day. Do you think we're really studying Torah here? Then let me tell you that we were simply unable to study because of our hunger. Can we attempt to combat healthy, overfed Gentiles?

Reb Mayshe. And what shall become of the Lord's holy cause?

The Stout One. A great cause indeed, but we're really unsuited to it.

The Thin One. Ach, ach, ach!

The Stout One. What's the use of talking? The moment we hear the first noise, we'll disappear from the synagogue.

Reb Mayshe. Woe is me. What do I hear? — As I blessed you before, so will I now curse you! You are wicked Jews, who defile the synagogue worse than the desecrating hands of Gentiles. What do you seek here? Your studying is an insult to Heaven, your praise of the Lord is blasphemy. Out of my sight, or I'll raise my ax first against your heads! Out with you, desecrators! [The Thin One *moves to the other side of the pulpit.*]

The Stout One [*retreating*]. Just the same, you needn't holler so, Reb Mayshe. You're not the whole boss here. [*Joins* The Thin One.]

Reb Mayshe [*struggling with his anger*]. And for these cowards I thanked you, O God! — Lord, where are your Jews? Where are your Jews, O Lord? You made me a preacher, to spread your word among the Jews, to teach them your commandments and win you their hearts. With all my soul I spoke to them untiringly, and now I stand before you, and must ask " Where are your Jews, Lord? Where is your army? " Reveal them to me, or take me to you. I can do no more, dear God! [*Hides his face in the curtain. Then, in a stifled voice.*] Jews, where are you? Jews, where are you? —[*He arises.*] God, have *you* sent such a thought to me? Does it come from you? [*Spreading his arms apart.*] I go. I'll search through the streets; I'll knock at every door. Jews, God's house is in danger!

Jews, desecrators want to sully our holy possessions! Lord, you have comforted me, and gladness fills my heart. I have lived my long life for this day alone. Even as Mattathias, son of Johanan the High Priest, so will I to-day assemble all the faithful Jews to wage war in defense of their holy symbols. No, I do not stand alone, a sole survivor. I am a pioneer, an organizer. Thanks to you, O Lord, who chose me for the glorious task! With armies, great armies, will I return to your house. The timorous shall glow with courage, the weak shall become strong. Be my guide, O Lord! I go! He who is with God, follow me! [*Goes out, with a firm step. The idlers make way for him, running over to the other side of the pulpit.*]

CURTAIN

SECOND SCENE

BANKER HERSHMAN'S *study. The floor is covered with large rugs. At the left center a library table, upon which lie various papers and books, very neatly arranged. Against the left wall a large safe. Between the safe and the table an arm-chair. On the other sides of the table three chairs. The right wall is taken up entirely with wide, well-stocked bookcases. At the rear, the door. In the left foreground a rocking-chair. Upon the left wall hang large portraits of the Russian Czar and his Czarina; on the right, pictures of noted Jews.*

YOUNG HERSHMAN *is seated upon the commodious rocking-chair, without a hat, picking his teeth and reading a paper. At the right stands the* RABBI *with one of the* DAYONS. *They are looking at the backs of the books in the cases. The* Second Dayon *is seated upon one of the chairs near the desk. He sits sideways, as if he were suffering from a physical irritation.*

The Rabbi [*admiring the books*]. Fine books! Excellent volumes!

First Dayon. P-p-precious c-c-collection!

Young Hershman [*from behind his paper*]. For appearances' sake, gentlemen. Merely for the sake of appearances! Just for the looks of the thing. They're never opened. Neither those in the book-case, nor these on the table here. Since I can remember, he's never even opened the bookcase. Except to put different books on the table and put the old ones back in the case.

First Dayon. You m-mustn't t-t-tell t-t-tales out of s-s-school, es-specially about your own f-father.

Young Hershman. If it's the truth, a person may tell it even about his father.

The Rabbi [*flatteringly*]. What a worthy son!

Second Dayon. But Mr. Hershman is a man who carries a good many affairs upon his mind.

The Rabbi [*still looking at the books*]. Fine books! Excellent collection!

Hershman [*enters. Goes over to the armchair*]. I presented the soldiers with some of our Passover wine, so that they'd have more patience standing guard over the house. [*Sits down.*] Isn't that fine of His Excellency? Eh? To send me five soldiers? People will surely imagine that some big general lives here. Ha-ha. — Well, gentlemen, be seated and . . . [*To his son.*] As for you, sit and listen and keep silent. And don't mix into our discussion. Otherwise, you may be off this moment.

YOUNG HERSHMAN [*from behind his papers*]. Ahem!
[THE RABBI *sits down near* HERSHMAN. *The two* DAYONS *sit down opposite each other.*]

HERSHMAN. Now then, gentlemen.— As I said before, I invited you to my house not merely that you should not be in your own unprotected homes during these dangerous hours and have something evil befall you,— God forbid — that, of course, was an important consideration. But I wanted chiefly to discuss with you a very weighty matter that concerns most intimately the Jewish race and its religion. I am therefore doubly sorry that my servant did not find Reb Mayshe at home. First, I am afraid lest he meet with some misfortune; second, his counsel would be very valuable to us now.

THE RABBI. Let us hope to God that no misfortune will overtake him. Perhaps he is hidden in some secure place, and God willing, when the danger is past, we'll be able to discuss matters with him.

HERSHMAN [*somewhat impatiently*]. Very well. . . . As I have said, naturally my heart swells with grief at thought of the pogrom. It was not necessary; it should not have been permitted to occur. I leave out of consideration those unfortunates who will suffer directly from it. A goodly number of Jews will perish, and perhaps more will be wounded and robbed. I leave all that out of consideration. I am looking into the future. Who knows better than I what sufferings are in store for us directly after the pogrom? Poverty will be more widespread; credit will be at a standstill, business establishments will go bankrupt. Not only in our city, but in many others where Jews are in business. In a word, times will be bad, merciful God. But, as I have said,— and this is the main point — our Jews are alone to blame. What says the Book? " But Jeshurun waxed fat, and kicked." They became too prosperous and lusted for more and more.

THE RABBI. That's exactly what I'm always arguing.

FIRST DAYON. Wh-wh-o doesn't know th-that? Wh-who d-doesn't s-see it?

YOUNG HERSHMAN [*with pious chanting*]. And perhaps it's just the contrary? Perhaps it's because things are going too badly with them?

SECOND DAYON. There's some truth in that, too.

HERSHMAN. I know what I'm talking about. Things are going altogether too well with them. That's why they raised their heads too high, and from this comes all their sorrows. Who knows this better than I? I hear our Jews spoken of very often,— in the highest circles, you'll understand,— in the very highest,— and I tell you, it puts me to shame. Upon my word of honor, it puts me to shame! [THE RABBI *and the* DAYONS *sigh.*] Not long ago I had a conversation with His Excellency. And he says to me, " With all my kindness of heart . . ."

YOUNG HERSHMAN [*sighs ironically from behind his papers*]. Ah! Ah!

HERSHMAN [*looking sternly at his son*]. "With all my kindness of heart," he said, "and with all my good will toward them, I simply can't endure your Jews. They are altogether," he says to me, "altogether too insolent. They say," he says to me, "that Jews are timorous. And I maintain," says he, "that they're altogether too bold. They're not timid enough," says he. "Fear," he says, "fear, fear, is just what they lack. And we'll have to teach them," says he, "to be afraid."

SECOND DAYON. Well, well. They'll learn to be afraid presently, all right.

HERSHMAN. Now what could I reply to his words? "I know," said I, "that we have black sheep among us,"

to defend them. Do you expect me, in such a crisis, to
wait till your servant announces me? Every minute is
precious, and I've already lost too many running to the
rabbi and the dayons.— Why do you stop to argue
with me, good heavens! The synagogue and the scrolls
are in danger!

HERSHMAN. Keep calm, my dear man. What would
you have us do?

REB MAYSHE. What would I have you do? Need I
wish it? Do you not know your duty? Do you not
know what God asks of you, in this moment? Keep
calm, you say? Lord of Abraham!

THE RABBI. But really, in truth. What are we to do
about it?

REB MAYSHE. Need I tell you? You must defend
the synagogue! You must protect the Holy Scroll with
your lives!

YOUNG HERSHMAN [*bursts out laughing*]. Fine!
There's talk for you!

REB MAYSHE. Laughter? Laughter at such a time?

HERSHMAN. How can anybody help laughing at you,
Reb Mayshe? You've taken something into your head
and don't know yourself what you want. Who is to run
to the defense of the synagogue? I? The Rabbi?
The Dayons?

REB MAYSHE [*with stern emphasis*]. You! The
Rabbi! The Dayons! Who else, then, if not you as
leaders? Do you stop to question? Mr. Hershman!
Reb Henzel! Dayons!

HERSHMAN. Are you joking, Reb Mayshe?

THE RABBI. Hm!

REB MAYSHE. Woe is me! Woe! [*Stands in stupefaction.*]

SECOND DAYON. I understand his meaning all right. But to tell the truth I've been suffering so much lately that I can barely stand on my feet.

REB MAYSHE. I . . . joking . . . ? Mr. Hershman, Gabbai, how can you mention such a thing? Dayons! Do not your hearts bleed to behold the danger that hovers over our holy possessions? Pious Jews, overseers of our faith, do not your fists instinctively double up against the desecrators of our Holy Scroll? No, *you* must be joking with *me*. But I warn you, delay not, lest it be too late. This is no time for jest or for bandying words. We need deeds. Come! He who is with God, follow me!

YOUNG HERSHMAN [*bursts once more into laughter*].

HERSHMAN [*motioning to his son*]. Sh-sh! — Listen to reason, Reb Mayshe. That's a fine slogan — " He who is with God, follow me " — Excellent. But, Reb Mayshe, pardon my saying it, you speak rank nonsense. Why, only just before you came in we were saying that something must be done, — something far, far more important to the Jewish community. If you're willing, calm down and we'll talk it over. I sent for you only a little while ago, but your house was closed.

REB MAYSHE. Is this a time for talking? How can I be calm when the synagogue is in danger? How can you talk so cold-bloodedly, and so calmly, when at this very moment foul hands may be desecrating our holy of holies? Talk! Come, I tell you. Offend not the Almighty!

HERSHMAN. Well, if you refuse to come to your senses, and persist in shouting your same old song, there's no use talking to you any further. But I tell you that the execution of our plan is far more important and necessary to our synagogues and our holy scrolls and to the whole Jewish people. We are evolving a plan that will protect our holy scrolls and synagogues forever, that will preserve our entire Judaism from ruin, and return our Torah and our faith to their ancient beauty and their honor of yore.

REB MAYSHE. Must and can your plan be executed at once?

HERSHMAN. It is a far-reaching plan, Reb Mayshe, extending into years and generations. . . .

REB MAYSHE. Then let your plan wait for later, till to-morrow or the day after, for years and for generations, and come now to defend the synagogue!

HERSHMAN. Why have you taken it into your head, Reb Mayshe, that we should rush to certain death . . . ?

REB MAYSHE. To glorious martyrdom!

HERSHMAN. . . . And leave our plan . . .

REB MAYSHE. . . . For our survivors to carry forward!

HERSHMAN. We must not do that. We do not know who the survivors will be.

REB MAYSHE. They will be Jews! Strengthened and inspired by our heroic death, they will be strong Jews!

HERSHMAN. That's mere talk. I maintain that the strong Jews, the true ones, will be massacred, only to have the evil ones, the dross, the apostates and the renegades remain. What will then become of our faith and our Holy Scroll? And above all, what shall we have gained by it? Let's suppose we go to defend the synagogue,— all of us, great heroes. I, you, the Rabbi, Reb Aaron and Reb Zissel. And what will be the result? We'll be slaughtered, the synagogue will be demolished anyway, and the scrolls desecrated. Isn't that so?

THE RABBI. How could it be otherwise?

FIRST DAYON. P-precisely s-so!

Reb Mayshe. Not at all! It is possible to desecrate the scrolls only when Jews refuse to defend them! In their being abandoned lies the real shame. In their being forsaken dwells their real debasement. But when Jews are ready to die for them, they cannot be desecrated, even if our enemies sully them in the most degrading manner. We must wipe off their stains with our blood, and they will emerge a thousandfold more clean. Their honor will grow and great will be their name. That is the glorious secret of martyrdom.

Second Dayon. True words!

Reb Mayshe. Pillars of the Torah, hide not behind your plan! Come to yourselves! Come to God! Brothers, if we cannot live like Jews, let us at least die like Jews!

Hershman. What do you mean —" we cannot live like Jews "? We *must* do so! That's just why we want to live!

Reb Mayshe [*sternly*]. Hide not behind your plans!

Hershman. Don't shout at me like that, Reb Mayshe! And whom do you take us for, that you presume to tell us not to hide behind our plans? Do you mean to insinuate that our plan is a hoax? A pretext? Are we hypocrites? Need we be afraid of you and court your favor?

Reb Mayshe. God, give me persuasion, give me speech, send me words! Guide me!

Hershman. You should have prayed for that long ago. Then perhaps your sermons would have had better effect, and indifference would not be so rife among Jews, and we wouldn't have had this pogrom.

Second Dayon [*smacks his lips in reproof of* Hershman].

Reb Mayshe. Lord God of Abraham! Shall I weep?

Shall I curse? Shall I implore? [*In tears.*] Jews, God's house is in danger! Jews, vandals want to desecrate our Torah! Jews,— you are called the worthy pillars of the Holy Law, will you not defend it? The precious Scroll, the loving, tender, sweet depository of our faith, will be alone when it is fallen upon by the desecrators! It will be alone, abandoned and forsaken, — and it will be torn, spat upon, soiled, trampled under foot! Woe is me! Torn, forsaken . . . our Torah, our one remaining glory! Pillars of the Holy Law, why do you hesitate? How can you bear to sit secure in the protection of soldiers, concocting plans, and leave the synagogue to its fate? Lay aside your plans! Judaism will be saved without you. Now the synagogue must be saved. With what heart will you later enter the ruined building, when you recall that it might have been rescued, but lacked defenders? With what eyes will you behold the torn and sullied sacred pages that will be still more sullied by the fact that you deserted them in their need? With what tongue will you speak to the people about Judaism, and the Holy Law and our Lord, when you, who should have been the first to protect the Holy Law, were the first to forsake it? You overseers of Judaism, God has entrusted a sacred duty to you — what will your answer be when He calls you to account? Woe, that I should have to tell you this! Rabbi, Gabbai and Dayons, bethink yourselves! To-day is your day! The day for you to show that you have earned your distinction as Rabbi, Gabbai and Dayons of the Jewish people! This is your day of martyrdom, the day on which you can glorify the name of our Lord, the honor of our Holy Law and the name of our people! Why do you still hesitate? What are you waiting for? Let us be off! Let us run. . . .

YOUNG HERSHMAN [*laughing sarcastically*]. Ah, Reb Mayshe, my dear Reb Mayshe, you've lived so many years and aren't any wiser yet. What nonsense have you talked into yourself? What synagogue must be defended, and what " sacred " scrolls? The synagogue in which ostentatious Jews fight for religious honors? In which they're not ashamed to raise the most disgraceful scandals, in which they drink whisky at death-anniversaries, as if they were in a tavern? The " sacred " scrolls which are written by Michel, the scribe, and which have been desecrated a thousand times already, during the services? What have you taken into your head, Reb Mayshe? Whom do you expect to risk his life to-day for such things? Why do you make of yourself a fool and a saint?

REB MAYSHE [*looks at the others in amazement, but they avoid his glance*]. Gentlemen, are you silent? Do you permit that blasphemer to open his mouth, and bear it mutely without rising in fury and stopping his shameful lips!

HERSHMAN. You'd better shut up! I've told you a thousand times not to intrude!

SECOND DAYON. That was really a disgraceful impertinence.

HERSHMAN. And to you, Reb Mayshe, let me say that we've had enough of your farce. To you, the synagogue is most important; to us, Judaism. And let there be an end to all this.

REB MAYSHE. Lord of Israel, now will I curse! I can do no more. Dear God, you have given me tears and soft words, now give me stones and lances and spleen! As your synagogue and your scrolls are abandoned and forsaken by them, even so may they be forsaken and abandoned, without any one to console them or to mourn them. May the shame that will be done to your holy gifts descend upon their heads and deliver their names to mockery and scorn. May the mire in which your holy scrolls will be trampled eat into their bodies and souls, so that neither water nor all the fires of hell be able to cleanse it!

HERSHMAN. The man's gone crazy, upon my word.

REB MAYSHE. Woe upon your heads, worthies of the Law, to whom the Holy Law is but a mask,— a matter of business. God's wrath descend upon you, dissemblers, hypocrites!

HERSHMAN [*angrily pounding the table with his fist*]. Reb Mayshe!

THE RABBI. What is this! What words are these?

REB MAYSHE. Dear God, not in mansions are your Jews to be found, and not under the fur-caps of the rabbis. I have gone astray, dear Father, and have taken the wrong path. But I will find your Jews; I will yet assemble your host. The day is yet long. Sun, do not set. I must find Jews. God, protect your house! [*Hurries out.*]

YOUNG HERSHMAN [*laughing*]. There goes a fanatic!

HERSHMAN. Mad. Stark mad. But he'll be our preacher no more.

SECOND DAYON [*with lowered eyes*]. I, too, am afraid he'll no more be a preacher. [*With tears in his voice.*] We may well mourn him, for he goes to a sure death. [*The others lower their gaze, their foreheads furrowed in thought. A deep silence.*]

CURTAIN

ACT III

A large clearing in the woods, approached from the right by a narrow path. In the foreground, center, lies MINYE, *resting against the stump of a tree. At her side sits* LEON, *his face buried in his hands, his hat on the grass nearby. In the background a group of Jews reading Psalms in subdued, tearful voices. In the front sits* YEKEF; *behind, among the trees, many women and children, choking with tears and using their handkerchiefs freely. The atmosphere is filled with a sad funereal stir. The entire crowd is much frightened; people often turn about suddenly, fear in their eyes, and at the slightest noise there is general terror.*

MINYE [*after a long pause*]. Speak to me, Leon. I am afraid I shall go mad. [LEON'S *head sinks lower.*] Speak to me, my son. Have you nothing to say to your mother? — I feel that I am at the end of my strength. Ah, Lord of the universe, where are they now? Where are they now? Are they still among the living? — Speak to me; say something; don't leave me alone with my thoughts; don't abandon me to the tortures of my imagination.

LEON. What can I say to you, mother?

MINYE. What can you say to me? My son, my son! I can't remember the time that you spoke with me. You lived under my roof, a stranger. I knew nothing of your sorrows or your joys,— just as if I were dead to you.

And I used to look at you, even as now,— to try and understand whether you really were my son, my little Leon. Was it really you that nestled in my bosom and sucked my milk and blood? Heaven, how many nights have I lain awake for you! What have I not suffered and endured for you — through all your illnesses and I know not what else, until I brought you to manhood. And now — you're as nothing to me,— a stranger! And to tell the truth, I feel a certain fear of you. But what's the use of talking? It's my lot, I suppose. Perhaps I deserve no better. But now, do try and think of something to say to me. You are a wise man, educated,— you are a writer. Speak to me, my son; speak to me. [*Places her hands about her head, which she shakes in deepening despair.*]

LEON. You'll not understand me, mother dear. You'll not understand.

MINYE. Then speak so that I may understand. Do you think me such a fool, then? Tell me, explain to me why we are such strangers to one another. Why can't I understand you? Speak to me, Leon. Speak to me.

LEON. Not to-day, mother. Not to-day.

MINYE [*restraining her tears.*] Let it be so, then.

LEON [*after a brief pause, burying his head in his hands*]. Mother, when we come home I'll explain all my writings to you. I'll translate and discuss every word, and then,— you'll make a large fire and help me burn a goodly part, if not all, of what I have written. Both verse and prose.

MINYE [*shakes her head despairingly and weeps. Meanwhile the praying has stopped.* YEKEF *comes over to his wife and son*].

YEKEF. Leon, perhaps you'll join us in the sunset prayers. Come, take your hat. We need only you for a minyan.[1] [LEON *does not notice his father.*] Do you hear me or not? With you we'll have just ten men. Obey your father this once.— You know that for a long time I've never spoken a word to you on these matters. Come now. [LEON *does not move.* YEKEF *continues with more earnest entreaty.*] I would not ask you, but what are we to do if you are the only one that can complete the minyan? Come, won't you?— It will be a shame to go back and tell them that you refuse. [LEON *is motionless.*] Well, what do you say to this, Minye? Fine, eh? Beautiful, eh?

MINYE. Didn't you know that before?

YEKEF. If I wouldn't restrain myself, I'd . . . I'd . . . See, they're beginning to pray already. What will they say of me now, I ask you? Fine, eh? Excellent, eh? See, they've come to the Eighteen Benedictions.[2] Would that a curse overtook all my children on the same day!

MINYE. Madman! You don't know what you speak! Better go and say your prayers with the others.

YEKEF. I . . . I . . . I'll . . .

REB MAYSHE [*from within. His voice comes from a distance, from the direction of the path*]. Jews! God's house is in danger! Jews! Vandals want to desecrate the Holy Scroll! [*The murmuring of the prayers stops suddenly. All listen, terror written upon their faces. The voice of* REB MAYSHE *comes nearer.*] Jews! God's house is in danger! Jews! Vandals want to desecrate our Holy Scroll!

MINYE. That's father's voice.

[1] The quorum of ten males above the age of thirteen required for all religious services. Jews keep their heads covered during all prayers.

[2] These are prayed in silence, standing, and must not be interrupted by speech upon the part of the worshipper.

YEKEF [*trembling*]. Yes! I would swear it's my father!

LEON [*who has arisen, and has looked through the trees*]. Yes, it's grandpa.

MINYE. Oh! What can be the matter with him? [*Those who are at prayer stand in mute terror. The women gather the children about them.*]

REB MAYSHE [*his voice is now very near*]. Jews! God's house is in danger! Jews! Vandals want to desecrate our Holy Scroll!

MINYE [*whispering to* YEKEF]. In God's name, don't mention a word to him about your brother's family having gone over to the Christians!

REB MAYSHE [*runs in, disheveled, gasping*]. Ah! Here they are! Thanks, O God, that you have brought me here! — Jews, do you hear? Quickly! Let's run, the synagogue is threatened, — we must save our sacred possessions! Jews, there is no time to lose! [*The men in the praying group begin to sway piously back and forth, and with exaggerated piety they move their lips in silent prayer. Those who have prayer-books suddenly bury their glances in them; those who have none close their eyes tight. The women commence to weep loudly and blow their noses.* REB MAYSHE *looks about.*] What! Oh, yes, I see. They're reciting the Eighteen Benedictions.

YEKEF. If you had come here just a moment sooner we should have had a minyan.

REB MAYSHE [*Does not look at* YEKEF. *Speaks more firmly*]. Jews, I absolve you. I authorize you to interrupt the Eighteen Benedictions. The synagogue stands alone, and the enemy is near. God needs you now. Come. You can pray in the synagogue. Why do

you stand still there, brothers? Do you hear what I say
to you? Do you understand what God asks of you?
The synagogue awaits the army of the Lord. Come!
[*The men at prayer sway to and fro more piously than
ever.* REB MAYSHE *looks about in astonishment.*] I
behold pious Jews,— eyes that will not open during the
Eighteen Benedictions, lips that whisper so religiously.
[*The men become more absorbed than ever in their
prayers.*] But have you ears that hear God's call?
Hearts that feel God's will? [*With emphasis.*] Do
you hear what I am saying to you, or not? Give me a
token that you hear. [*The men sway to and fro, and
continue to mumble their prayers.*]

YEKEF [*moves away from* REB MAYSHE *and begins
to pray the Eighteen Benedictions. He closes his eyes*].

MINYE [*breaks suddenly into hysterical weeping*].

REB MAYSHE. Brethren, Jews, listen to me. Close
your mouths and open your ears. Open your eyes and
your hearts. See and hear and feel that God is calling
you now. His house waits for you. [*To a yellow-faced
Jew.*] Brother Jew, you're tall and broad and strong,
and you pray with such fervor. Come, show God that
you serve Him truly. Come, show Him that you can
sacrifice all to His glorious name when He asks it. Stop
your prayers, I demand it! Come, I say. I'll stop
them for you. [*Pulls the man away.*] Come, you are
strong.

THE YELLOW JEW [*attempting to free himself from*
REB MAYSHE]. Nu! Oh! Ah!

THE YELLOW JEW'S WIFE [*rushes forth from among
the trees, one child in her arms and two weeping tots
following her*]. Why have you singled him out from
all the rest? Aren't there plenty of other men here?
Why don't you take your own son away? There he

stands, too, praying away so piously. Never mind my husband. He's got a family to defend.

THE YELLOW JEW [*tearing himself away and casting an angry look at* REB MAYSHE]. Ah! [*Resumes praying.*]

THE YELLOW JEW'S WIFE [*returns to her place among the trees*]. Did you ever see? He drags men away! God has nobody else to fight His battles except my husband,— a father of three small children!

REB MAYSHE [*who has looked about beseechingly, of a sudden raises his voice*]. Jewish sons, Jewish daughters! Do you know what martyrdom means? Our Lord has many peoples, but one alone has He chosen. To that one He entrusted His Holy Law and made it the guardian. And therefore He said to His people: "Protect my holiness with the blood of your hearts, with your body and soul. Let nothing be more to you; be ready to sacrifice all in its defense. Thus will you reveal to all the nations the power of my holiness, and will render my name great and sacred. And all peoples will recognize my power and will know that I am the one and true God. This will be your greatest and only thanks for the gift I have made you and my blessing will descend upon you. But if you do not guard it with the blood of your hearts, with your body and soul, and if you allow other things to become nearer and dearer to you, then will the nations that know me not desecrate my holiness and insult my name. But you alone will be the real desecrators; you alone will be my real defamers, yours alone will be the unclean hands, the impure heart and deeds. And I will hide my face and weep at the ingratitude of my chosen people, and will curse it forever." Jewish sons, Jewish daughters! Not with pious mumbling and closing of your eyes can you thank

God and please Him, and move His heart, but only with the glorification of His name among the peoples of the Earth. This is such a day, my children! Seize the opportunity! Bethink you who you are! Remember that you are Jews! Strengthen your hearts and come! Holiness awaits you. Jews! Jews!

[THE MEN *continue their pious swaying and mumbling.*]

REB MAYSHE [*speaks now with an exhausted voice*]. Lord of the universe, what now can I say? What more can I add? [*Looks around him again with entreaty and despair.*] Jewish children, to-day I was told that Judaism had departed from the world, that there were no more pious Jews, that I was a solitary survivor. But I laughed at the blasphemers. "Israel is not a widower," I told them. There are still among us pious Jews without number. Answer me, did I speak the truth or not? [*Looks around for a reply.*] What? Has no one yet finished the Eighteen Benedictions? Are your prayers endless?

[THE MEN *continue their pious swaying and mumbling.*]

REB MAYSHE [*his voice becomes kind, tender and more feeble*]. Ah, my Jews, my Jews! When I left the blasphemers to-day, I hoped that I would find the synagogue thronged with Jews — old and young, men and women — a synagogue crowded with the army of the Lord. But I found the place empty, forgotten and forsaken. I fell before the Holy Ark and wept before God. I asked Him, where was His army, where were His Jews? Was I then really the only, the last Jew? And it was as if God's voice spoke to me: "Go and assemble my host. You will find it in vast numbers." And the Lord was with me and brought me in

safety to you, through hordes of the enemy. Do you
not feel that God meant you? Can you not see that the
Lord has chosen you for His army, to defend His house
and to protect His sacred gifts? . . . You are silent?
You sway and mumble still? Give me at least a sign
that when you have concluded the Eighteen Benedictions
you will follow me.

[THE MEN *continue their swaying and mumbling.*]

REB MAYSHE [*now speaks in very hoarse tones*].
Jews! In a few moments you can win a place in
Paradise! Follow me! Jews, who you are and what
you are, advance to sacrifice your lives for God's house
and for His holy gifts, and you will have purchased your
happiness in the next world. Follow me, Jews, to martyrdom!

[THE MEN *continue their swaying and mumbling.*]

REB MAYSHE [*looks about him in stupefaction and
meets* LEON's *glance. The latter, pale with emotion,
has been leaning against a tree; his face betrays deep
thought and amazement, as if he were beholding a
vision.* REB MAYSHE *looks at him with a penetrating
glance*]. What do my eyes behold? You are moved?
You, the sinner and the instigator of others' sins? You,
the Jeroboam son of Nebat?

[LEON *smiles weakly.*]

REB MAYSHE [*gazes for a while upon the praying
men*]. Brethren, I am waiting for you. [*To* LEON,
regarding him keenly.] Listen to a story from the Talmud. When Rome forbade Jews to study the Holy Law,
the learned preacher Hanino Tradinus paid no attention
to the decree and continued to discuss the Holy Law in
public. So they seized him and wrapped him in a Holy
Scroll and threw him upon a heap of fresh twigs, which
they lighted. His breast they covered with moist wool,

so that he would roast longer at the stake. The sage
suffered it all, but did not abjure the Torah. The executioner
beheld this and his heart was moved. He told
the sage to remove the wet wool, so that his death might
come more quickly. The sage, however, answered that
such an act would be equivalent to self-murder. The
executioner, at this, was even more moved by the learned
man's fortitude. He removed the wool from the burning
man's breast and himself jumped into the flames. And
both were soon burned to death. You, Leon, have always
been one of my executioners. Limb after limb you
slowly burned off me. Piece by piece, drop by drop you
have robbed me of my life. And now, now you are
moved by my plight and look upon me with kindly eyes.
Are you, perhaps, thinking of jumping into the flames
with me?

LEON [*hoarsely*]. No, grandpa. I must remain your
executioner,— the executioner of your world-philosophy,
of your faith, of your Holy Law, of your God. But I
marvel at you,— the man in you, the great beauty that
dwells in you, which I have never noticed till now,—
the remarkable power that I realize now for the first
time. As a tribute to you yourself I could fall on my
knees and kiss the hem of your cloak. For you yourself,
for the greatest of Jews, for the solitary and
last . . .

REB MAYSHE. Enough, enough! I want to hear no
more. You are a blasphemer, a blasphemer! [*To the
men.*] Did you hear his words? — What! You are
still in silent prayer? — God in Heaven, once again have
I strayed. I have blundered upon a den of cowardly
wretches, upon a lair of hypocrites and robbers of the
Lord. God of Abraham, surely I am not a solitary survivor?
Surely I am not the last Jew? I will yet dis-

cover your army! I will yet assemble defenders of your house and your holy gifts. Lead me, lead me upon the right path! Guide me to the right streets, show me the right houses! Dear God, I rely upon you! Lead me, lead me upon the right road! [*Hastens away over the path.*] Jews, where are you? Jews! God's house is in danger! Jews! Vandals want to desecrate our Holy Scroll! Where are you? Where are you? [*He disappears, and his voice is lost in the distance.*]

MINYE [*she has been weeping all this time. Cries out*]. Oh, we have seen him for the last time! For the last time we have seen him! [*The men still sway and mumble.*]

A WOMAN. A holy Jew.

THE YELLOW JEW'S WIFE. It's easy enough for him. He's lived his life. If he were a young man and the father of three little children, I'm not so sure whether he'd be such a saint.

[*A murmuring from* THE WOMEN: "That's so." . . . "She's right." . . . "No, no." . . . "Ah, well." . . . "Ah!" . . . THE MEN *at prayer end the Eighteen Benedictions and begin to pray aloud. They do not look at one another. There is an atmosphere of embarrassment.* MINYE'S *sobbing is heard.* LEON, *from his place by the tree, regards the crowd pensively.*]

THE YELLOW JEW. The gall of a man to grab me just when I was in the middle of the Eighteen Benedictions. Did you ever hear of a pious Jew doing a thing like that? [*There is no reply. The atmosphere of embarrassment still weighs heavily upon all.*]

LEON. But you're through with the Benedictions now. You heard his summons and you know where the synagogue is situated,— then why are you still standing here? Why don't you run to the synagogue?

First Jew. Behold! A new saint has arisen!

Second Jew. And when we needed him for a minyan he was deaf to our request!

Third Jew. And did you hear his parable? That he was the executioner of God and of the Torah? Hey?

Leon. Don't disguise your cowardice under the cloak of piety. Neither do I call upon you, nor do I tell you what you should do. But *you* are pious Jews, are you not? And the synagogue is *your* synagogue, and the holy scrolls are *your* sacred possessions. Look into your hearts; are you doing right? Do you not feel guilty,— that you are grievous sinners against your God?

Fourth Jew. Where were we at in the Psalms? [*The men sit down, ready to begin the recital of the Psalms.*]

Leon. Jews, you'll not drown out the voice of your conscience with your Psalm-saying. I tell you beforehand, the more you recite, the deeper will you feel your guilt.

Fifth Jew [*beginning Psalm Eighty-four*]. " To the chief Musician, upon Gittith. A Psalm for the sons of Korah."

Leon. Jews, listen to me.

[The Men *join the Psalm reader in chorus.*] " How amiable are thy tabernacles, O Lord of hosts."

Leon [*raises his voice above the sound of the others*]. Because my grandfather called you and you refused to go,— because the synagogue will be destroyed and the holy scrolls sullied, you will be the unhappiest of men. Never will you be able to find rest, never will you be able to find peace between you and your God. You will go about, your forehead branded with the mark of grievous sinners.

The Yellow Jew. Here's a new sermonizer for you!

YEKEF [*to* LEON]. What business is this of yours? Nobody's asking you what to do!

LEON. Gentlemen, hear me out. A few moments only.

THE MEN. "For a day in thy courts is better than a thousand . . ." [*The voices become weaker.*]

FIRST JEW. It's a sin to interrupt our service just for him.

LEON. For a moment only. [THE MEN *continue to recite the Psalm in a low voice, and* LEON *begins to talk somewhat excitedly.*] Gentlemen, you know very well that there are very few really pious Jews in the world, and when such a one dies, it must be in your eyes a great loss to all Israel. Jews, just now there went from you to his death one of the most pious of Jews,— in my opinion the only and last true Jew. If you permit him to die your Judaism will suffer an irreparable loss. Do your duty to Judaism. . . .

THE YELLOW JEW'S WIFE. Listen to him, will you! Prating of duty! We have enough duties, praised be God!

THIRD JEW. Hear the unbeliever! "Your" everything! "Your!" "Your" Judaism. . . . "Your" God. . . . "Your." . . . Hey?

THE YELLOW JEW. It's *his* grandfather, isn't it? Then why shouldn't *he* go and defend him?

LEON. I will. But to you he should be even more than a grandfather!

FIFTH JEW. Ah! What's the use? All nonsense. Let's resume our Psalms. [*They resume their reading.*]

LEON [*for a while regarding the group with scorn and disgust*]. And suppose I leave the woods and set the rioters upon you? [*The crowd, thunderstruck, gapes at him with distended eyes. Soon, however, there is a commotion, and the men jump to their feet.*]

YEKEF. What! What! What's that you said?
FIRST JEW. You blackguard! You infidel!
SECOND JEW. What spiteful notions can occur to a renegade!
THE YELLOW JEW. I'll strike you dead on the spot, you pesthole of wickedness!
FOURTH JEW. You won't live to get out of the woods!
VARIOUS WOMEN [*clasp their terrified, crying children, wring their hands and curse*]. Oh! May a plague enter all his bones!— Oh! May the cholera seize him!— May his legs break beneath him!— May he split his head! [*The crowd surges toward* LEON, *noisily and menacingly.* MINYE *arises from her place and steps toward him, as if to defend him.* LEON *speaks with all his strength.*] Order! [*The men halt and* LEON *speaks more calmly.*] I have a revolver here. Whoever raises his hand against me is a dead man! [*Turns away in disgust.*] Go back to your prayers. I'll not send anybody here after you. [*The men stand for a moment, eyeing* LEON *angrily, then turn back to their Psalms.*]
A VOICE. Such words a wicked man can utter! [MINYE *sinks helplessly back to her place.*]
LEON [*lifting his hat from the ground*]. I'm going, mother! Good-by. [*The men resume their Psalm-chanting.*]
MINYE [*in terror*]. You're going? You're really going?
LEON. I must help grandpa, mother. Be brave. Good-by.
MINYE [*resisting a hysterical outburst*]. Go, my son. — I — will — be brave. I'll not cry any more.— No, I'll not cry. [*Arises with great effort.*] Go, my son. But first let me kiss you . . . for all the long years. [*Bursts into hysterical weeping and falls against his*

bosom.] Oh, I'll never see you again! They will kill you! Oh! — All three in one day!

LEON [*moved*]. Be calm, mother dear. You said you would be brave. And that you wouldn't cry. Be calm. We'll see each other again. Let me be off. I may be too late.

MINYE [*strengthening herself*]. Go, my son. Go. And may God . . . my God will . . .

LEON [*kisses her*]. Well,— Good-by. [*Rushes away.*]

MINYE. Leon! One moment. . . . Leon, for my sake. . . . Leon, say good-by to your father.

LEON [*calls back as he hastens away*]. Good-by, father! [*Disappears among the trees.*]

MINYE [*calling after him*]. Leon, one thing more. . . . Leon, only a moment. . . . Leon, be sure to . . . Leon, be sure to pray . . . The death-prayer, "Hear, O Israel!"

ACT IV

SCENE ONE

A square before the synagogue. To the right, the high entrance to the house of worship; to the left, and in the background, houses. The left row of dwellings is intersected, in the rear, by a lane that leads to the synagogue; to the right, in front of the synagogue, another lane.— The square is absolutely deserted; the house-gates, doors and shutters are closed. From afar is heard the sound of many voices, coming gradually nearer.

REB MAYSHE [*his cry of relief is heard from the little street in the right foreground*]. The synagogue is still safe! The synagogue is safe! [*Comes rushing in. His cloak is torn; on his left temple there is blood, and his beard has been plucked in places. Runs into the synagogue and is soon out again.*] Thanks be to you, dear God! You have shielded your house. . . . But what have I done for it? Alone I departed from it, and alone I return. . . . Dear God! Where is your army? The enemy is near, and your army has not yet appeared.— Or will you defend your house unaided? Will you hurl down upon the foe your lightning and your thunderbolts? Dear God, I pray you, I do not want your thunder; send not your lightning. Send me your host; I want your Jews, dear God! I want your Jews to stand up for your house and your holy gifts,— to show that you still live within them,— that they serve you with love and with all their hearts and that they still are ready to sacrifice themselves for you. It is they that I want. [*He prostrates himself upon the steps that lead to the synagogue.*] I know that you alone, Almighty God, can save the synagogue! I know that you need none to take your part. But with tears and with entreaty I implore you, send me your Jews. Show me where they are! — Or take me back to you. I no longer care to live! I no longer care to live! [*Begins to sob but soon restrains himself. He sits up, and speaks in a feeble, tearful voice.*] Jews! Jews! Where are you? [*Arises, steps out into the middle of the square, looks about, and calls, in a voice choked with tears.*] Jews! God's house is in danger! Jews! God's house is in danger! Assemble, Jews! Assemble, army of the Lord! Crawl forth from your hiding-places. Crawl out of your holes, your cellars and your attics. Arise, Jews, to your holy task! [*Walks over to the house in the left foreground, dries his eyes with his wide sleeve, knocks at the door, and cries out, somewhat more firmly.*] Into the synagogue, Jews! Into the synagogue! Reb Sholom Yankev, the house of worship is alone. Come out, Reb Sholom Yankev! It's I, Mayshe, the preacher. The enemy is near, and the synagogue is alone. But we must not leave it undefended, Reb Sholom Yankev. I surely need not tell that to you, for you are a pious Jew.— No voice, no reply.— [*Knocks louder.*] Have you died of fright in there? [*Raps against the shutters.*] Do you hear me, Jewish children? The synagogue is deserted, God's house is in danger! [*From the lane at the left comes the sound of some one running towards the square.* REB MAYSHE *hastens to the steps of the synagogue and looks in the direction of the footsteps.*] A Jew, a Jew running . . . and he's hastening hither. . . . God, dear God! . . . [*A Jew of some thirty-odd years, with a long beard and wearing a felt hat, comes running in towards the synagogue. When he beholds* REB MAYSHE *he takes fright and recoils; soon recognizing the preacher, however, he continues to run, and rushes up the steps into the synagogue.* REB MAYSHE'S *voice reveals gratified delight.*] Heavenly Father! One soldier has already arrived. Thanks, O Lord. And now, one after the other.

THE JEW IN THE SOFT HAT [*coming back to the door of the synagogue*]. The synagogue is empty!

REB MAYSHE. Yes, my child. The synagogue is empty. God's army has not yet been mobilized.

THE JEW [*with a worried expression*]. Then of what use is the synagogue to me? I thought that I'd surely find a big crowd in the synagogue, and that somehow or other, in a crowd one's fear wouldn't be so great.

REB MAYSHE [*with fright*]. You were concerned with yourself, then, and not with the synagogue?

THE JEW [*coming down the steps, perplexed*]. And where can I hide now? [REB MAYSHE *buries his face in his left arm.*] Advise a man, Reb Mayshe. Where can I hide now?

REB MAYSHE. Away from me! Crawl under the synagogue.— There you will find some other pigs, too.

THE JEW [*regards* REB MAYSHE *with astonishment, then looks under the synagogue. As if to himself*]. What do you think? It's really a splendid place. [*Disappears under the steps.*]

REB MAYSHE. Dear God, once more you have deceived me; once more roused false hopes in my bosom. Lord of the universe, if it pleases you to toy with me, then play whatever prank you please. But I pray you, let this jest soon come to an end. If you have appointed me mobilizer of your army, then let me assemble it at once. If not now, when then? The enemy is fast approaching; his shouting, excited by brandy and the taste of Jewish blood, comes nearer and nearer. Come to my aid, Almighty Father! Come to my aid! [*Drying his tears with his sleeve.*] Jews! Into the synagogue! The synagogue is in danger! Vandals want to desecrate our Holy Scroll! Jews! Arise to your holy task! [*Begins to knock at the door of the second house to the left.*] Jewish children! Come to the aid of God's house! Help! Help! The synagogue calls to you! [*From the little street at the right comes the sound of footsteps.* REB MAYSHE *stops his knocking at the door and listens.*

A POOR OLD JEWISH WOMAN [*approaches the steps of the synagogue, beholds* REB MAYSHE, *for a while stands still, shakes her head and utters a strange cry of grief. She mounts the steps*].

REB MAYSHE [*speaks with a frightened voice*]. It's the dumb, half-crazy beggar-woman! [*The* BEGGAR-WOMAN *disappears inside the synagogue.* REB MAYSHE, *for a few moments, looks toward the entrance to the synagogue with gaping eyes, as if waiting for something. His voice rises to an excited pitch.*] Lord God of Abraham, you have carried your jest too far! Of all your people you have sent to me only the dumb, half-crazy beggar-woman. This is too much,—too much! [*Falls against the banister of the stairs, his face buried in his left arm. Soon he arises, in a pensive, distraught mood.*] Have you sent a sign to me? How shall I interpret it? What do you mean by it? Dear God, can you not see that I am too small to understand you? [*From the left background comes the sound of footsteps.* REB MAYSHE *raises his glance and cries out with a note of hope in his voice.*] A Jew comes running hither! Are you sending him to me? Was the other but a beginning? [*A Jew of some thirty years, wearing a cap and having a small beard, appears at the rear and is about to run through the little street there.*]

REB MAYSHE [*blocking his path*]. Where are you running to, Mr. Jew? The synagogue is right here.

THE JEW WITH THE CAP [*recoils, begins to tremble all over, and retreats slowly. His face wears the expression of a madman*]. Oh! Oh! Don't kill me! Oh! Oh! Dear master, my dear master! Oh! Oh! Don't kill me! [*Falls upon his knees*]. I am a poor man, a poor, wretched Jew. What,— what do you want of me? Oh! Oh! Let me live! My master, my dear, dear master, don't kill me. I have nothing, nothing, nothing!

REB MAYSHE. Come to your senses, my dear fellow. Don't you see who's standing before you? It's I, Reb Mayshe the preacher.

THE JEW [*still retreating*]. Oh! Oh! Don't kill me! Don't kill me! I haven't anything. . . . My dear master, I've got nothing, nothing. . . . Master, master. . . . Oh! Oh! Oh! [*He turns suddenly around and rushes off with a wild shrieking.*]

REB MAYSHE. He's gone mad . . . gone mad because of me. My God, why have you done this? God in Heaven, how am I to interpret this? . . . Are you testing me? Are you trying to discover whether such a thing will deter me from fulfilling your mission? Lord of the Universe, I swear to you that you have done this in vain! Nothing shall deter me! In vain have you failed to take pity upon your creature. Nothing shall hold me back! Masterful and gracious Lord, why did you do this? Why? [*Stands for a moment with eyes raised to heaven;*

soon he covers his eyes with his left arm, lowering his arm immediately.] You send me riddle upon riddle. No. I will not attempt to fathom you. Your will is great, your thoughts are inscrutable. I will do my duty. [*Turns to the houses and begins to knock at the doors.*] Quickly, Jews! The synagogue waits for you. It is deserted, and cries for defenders. Sons of Israel, hear you not the voice of God? He is calling you. Jews! God's house is in danger! Come forth from your holes! Into the synagogue! [*From the right background appears a young man arm in arm with a girl.*]

THE YOUNG MAN. Don't be afraid. Just walk a little faster.

THE GIRL. Yes, Lord of the universe. Anything, anything . . . let them do anything, except . . . .

REB MAYSHE [*coming before them*]. Jewish children, with the Lord of the universe upon your lips, here is the house of the Lord of the universe. Come and protect it.

THE YOUNG MAN [*angrily*]. You're a big fool, Mr. Preacher. In perilous times like these you've no business standing here on the street and frightening passers by. [*He is about to walk off with the girl.*]

REB MAYSHE. My son, I pardon the insult to me. I am here because I must be here,— because God has sent me hither. The synagogue stands alone and it must be defended. And I am assembling God's army for that purpose. Go in, Jewish children, enter to defend the honor of the Lord and of his Holy Scroll.

THE YOUNG MAN. I don't know what it is more important to protect: the honor of the Holy Scroll or that of a Jewish daughter. I'd rather defend the honor of a Jewish maiden.— Come, Rosie, quickly. We are already near. [*The* YOUNG MAN *and the* GIRL *make their way quickly to the left.*]

THE GIRL. Oh! Lord of the universe! Let them do anything, anything. . . . Let them break my bones, let them twist my arms, let them kill me,— but not that, not that. . . .

REB MAYSHE [*raises his eyes to heaven, spreads out his arms, and for a moment is lost in thought*]. What do you say, great Father? Which is more precious in your eyes? [*With a start.*] And must I ask such a question? Children! Wait a while! The Holy Scroll is the more precious,— the honor of the Lord is more worthy! Into the synagogue! [*Runs a few steps after the couple.*] They do not hear me. O God, I am a worthless leader. Perhaps the right words do not come to me. God, you are my witness, I am doing my best. You can see that my words, however poor they be, come from the depths of my heart. You can see into my heart, great Seer, you can see! Send me new words, that I may move their hearts! Lord, come to my aid! [*He goes to the left background and knocks at the doors of the houses there.*] Sons of Israel, dear, faithful Jewish children! God's house, the sacred synagogue with its holy scrolls is in dire necessity and has sore need of you, Jewish children. It is a sin to hide and leave the Lord's house undefended.— The house in which you spoke to God, whence you sent to Him your prayers and entreaties, you must not leave alone. Sweet, loving, faithful Jewish children, if you wish the Lord to hear your voice, then hear now His. Into the synagogue, children! [*Suddenly he breaks into a fearful, penetrating wailing.*] Oh! O-oh! O-oh! [*Rushes forward, his hands to his head.*] Woe to my eyes, what they have seen! An idol in a Jewish window! A cross painted on a Jewish door! Oh! Oh! God! Take me to you! Take me back to you! Or I'll commit something desperate against myself! I'll smash my head against the walls of your house! Righteous Judge, take me back to you! Let the walls of your synagogue crumble about my head. We both are superfluous here; we are both no longer needed. [*Shaking the banister of the stairs wildly.*] Woe, what I have looked upon! Woe, what I have seen! God, take me back to you! [*Prostrates himself upon the steps.*] Lord of the universe, what else now? What further? [*Jumps up.*] Oh! I know! Mattathias son of Johanan the High Priest first took vengeance upon the wicked man who was about to sacrifice a pig to the strange idol, and then he became the gatherer of the Lord's army. I will do likewise! Yes, I will do likewise! [*Begins to pick up stones from the street and runs to the houses in the left background. He begins to break the windows.*] Take that, you sinners! And that, — traitors to Israel! May the most wretched of deaths be yours, renegades! To me this instant! I'm waiting for you! With my own hand I'll batter your brains! Vile creatures! You've put an idol in your window and hidden yourselves! But my stones will strike you none the less, and God's thunder will reach you, and destruction will overtake you!

VOICES [*from the right background*]. Quickly! Quickly! They're smashing windows over there! [*Enter* REUBEN *with a band of young men.*]

REB MAYSHE [*triumphantly*]. I have but just avenged God, and already His army approaches. [*He comes over to* REUBEN *and the group of young men. Astonished.*] What! Is it Reuben? No, this is not God's army. Yet, perhaps — perhaps?

REUBEN. Grandpa, who was breaking those windows over there?

REB MAYSHE [*softly*]. I did that, my child. They

placed an idol there in the window, and painted a cross upon the door.

REUBEN [*to his men*]. Well, let's be on our way. [*Points to the right foreground, where the voices have become louder and nearer. The band of young men rush toward the right.*]

REB MAYSHE. Halt, Jewish children! I'll keep you but a moment. [*They come to a halt, unwillingly. Some of them rush forth as soon as* REB MAYSHE *begins to speak.*] Do you remember, when you were yet little school-boys, and some misfortune would befall you or your family, how you would come to the synagogue and stand in some corner, pouring out your little hearts to God? And then your hearts would become so light? Do you remember, Jewish children? And now, behold! That same synagogue is in dire need. It is forsaken and forgotten by all. There is no one to take its part. [*The group of men show signs of leaving.*] Patience, children, and let me finish. I know that long ago you broke with the synagogue, but are you not willing to thank it now for the favors it showed you in your childhood? Will you not now protect it?

ONE OF THE GROUP. What do you call this? Sermonizing? [*The group of men rushes forth.*]

REUBEN [*lingering*]. Grandpa, duty and necessity call us thither.

REB MAYSHE. Necessity calls you thither?

REUBEN. We must be where human lives are in danger, — where the few possessions of our poor people are being plundered and destroyed. Our duty is to disperse the rioters. But the open street is really no place for you.

REB MAYSHE. Go your way!

REUBEN [*after looking at him a moment*]. Let it be so, then. [*Rushes off.*]

REB MAYSHE. Necessity calls him *thither!* No! That is not your army, O Lord. I knew it at once. They have forgotten you entirely. They have made humanity — your creation — their God and they serve it. As for you, they have dethroned you entirely. . . . But where is your army? Where, dear God? [*Looks about as if he were seeking people. From the right comes the sound of whistled signals. From the left background is heard the patter of many feet.* REB MAYSHE *moves toward the synagogue, then stops and cries out.*] This way! Come this way, Jewish children! This is the right place! [LIPMAN *comes running in with a band of young men.*]

LIPMAN. What's the trouble, grandpa? Has it begun here already?

REB MAYSHE. No, Lipman. Nothing's been begun here. In this place something must be ended; it is here that the last battle must be fought. [*The whistled signals at the right sound louder. The young men rush in that direction.* REB MAYSHE *seizes* LIPMAN *and detains him.*] Lipman, if all those young men belong to your band, then call them back.

LIPMAN. What sort of whim do you call this? Don't you hear the signals and the voices shouting?

REB MAYSHE. I hear them, I hear them well. But I hear another voice, too, which you have not yet heard. I hear the voice of God. Call them back, I tell you. See, here stands God's house, deserted. Will you young men not protect it? You are Jewish patriots, are you not? Does not the Jewish God speak somewhere within you?

LIPMAN [*with heat*]. They're shedding Jewish blood over there while we talk! They're destroying Jewish property!

Reb Mayshe. Almost the very words that Reuben spoke to me, only you use the word "Jewish" where he used the term "human." But I tell you to call back your people. My dear child, here stands the holy pillar that has supported the Jewish people throughout its whole existence. Support and defend that pillar! If it falls, the whole Jewish folk falls with it!

Lipman. Is this a time for me to begin a philosophic discussion with you? The Jewish folk will continue to exist without your pillar. [*About to go.*]

Reb Mayshe. A moment more. In the olden times, when an enemy oppressed the Jews, all the enemy needed to do was to lay foul hands upon the Jewish faith, or upon its sacred Torah, and the Jews arose like a single man, joined forces and fought with the feeling that they were a united people. What can now bring you all together?

Lipman. The will to be a people.

Reb Mayshe. Without God? Without the Holy Law? Call back your men.

Lipman. Folly! [*Rushes off. As he reaches the corner of the little street in the foreground he stops.*] And what will become of you?

Reb Mayshe [*sobbing*]. Away from my sight!

Lipman. Hm! [*Disappears.— The noise and the shouting comes very near.*]

Reb Mayshe [*exhausted, drags himself to the steps, where for a while he stands, leaning against the banister. He sinks slowly upon a step, lost in thought*]. My mission is at an end. The enemy is near; it is already upon the synagogue. I can no longer leave the Lord's house. And where should I go, anyway? To whom shall I turn? [*Looks about.*] Nobody comes. Nobody's about. Dear God, am I then really a solitary survivor, an only and a last Jew? Has your army really deserted, and do there remain to you only the dumb and the mad? [*He is again lost in thought; he looks about once more and speaks in a feeble voice.*] Nobody comes. Nobody's about.— Reb Mayshe the preacher, are you still alive? Reb Mayshe the preacher, what does God want of you now? Your time has departed, your day draws to a close. See, the sun is setting. It is your sun that sets, — yours and your God's. [*With a start.*] Have I not sinned just now with such speech? What have I said! What have I said! Good God, what did I say just then! Can your sun set? Can your time depart? Eternal God, dear God, you will yet work your miracles! Masterful and gracious Lord, if you grant me life so that I may behold your miracles, then I want to live, and great is my thanks for every minute that I survive. [*The frightful cries of a multitude of voices are now very near.* REB MAYSHE *begins to mount the stairs.*] With joy and hope do I enter now your house. God, I await your miracles!

SCENE TWO

Interior of the synagogue. The windows glow with the red of the setting sun. From outside comes the wild noise of a mob.— In the right corner sits the dumb BEGGAR-WOMAN, *uttering from time to time a strange piercing wail.*

THE BEGGAR WOMAN [*beholding* REB MAYSHE *wails louder than ever*].

REB MAYSHE [*looks at her; then, with a sigh, mounts the altar and kisses the curtain, taking it with trembling hands and hiding his face in its folds. He opens the Holy Ark and kisses the sacred scrolls. The beggar woman follows every movement of his, and continues to wail loudly*]. Holy scrolls, precious parchments! There yet will appear those who will protect you! You will not have to suffer the greatest of outrages,— to be sullied in abandonment, forsaken and forgotten! Holy Torah, greatest of God's creations, stand before Him and pray that he send you at once His army. [*Buries his head in the parchments.*] Dear God, dear God! . . . Where is your miracle,— your miracle! [*For a while he remains thus; then he straightens himself, dries his tears, bends down to the bottom drawer of the Holy Ark and takes out prayer-shawls and surplices.*] See, dear God, I am preparing for those who are coming. And if there'll not be enough prayer-shawls and surplices, they who must go without them will surely not be less holy in your eyes. [*Puts on a surplice.*]

THE BEGGAR WOMAN [*runs up the altar, kisses the sacred scrolls and speaks in a dumb, futile wailing; kissing the scrolls again, she turns to* REB MAYSHE *with a pious expression, shaking her head, goes down from the altar and sits at the right of the Holy Ark, her gaze fixed upon* REB MAYSHE *as she continues to wail*].

REB MAYSHE [*has looked upon her actions with exaltation. He cries out*]. God, how strong you are in her! How great are you, O Lord, if fear of you dwells even in such a creature. If only all those who have denied you might gaze upon her here, how they would be filled with your majesty and with fear of your power! They would fall upon their knees and beat their breasts, praising your name and singing Psalms to your glory. . . . Dear God, is that why you sent her hither? Is that why you wish to have her here? . . . No, dear Lord, I beg you not to do it! I refuse to accept her from you. I do not want her. I want your Jews,— your Jews,— those who have speech and understanding.

I entreat you, Almighty Father, I ask no other message of you than them, only them. Show them, and show me, that I am not the only Jew nor the last one. Reveal to me that your army *is* still a vast one, that you yet dwell in countless hearts, and not only in the heart of this dumb, mad woman. Send me your army! The greater it will be, the brighter will shine the glory of your name. The more lives that offer themselves to the defense of your house, the holier and more powerful will you become. Dear God, surely you know this! Hear my prayers, Lord. Your miracle, dear God, your miracle! [*Outside there is a tumult and a noise of scurrying hither and thither. Stones come flying through the windows. One of them strikes* REB MAYSHE *in the temple, and he begins to bleed. He seizes the crowbar, raises it high above his head with both hands and takes his stand before the doors of the Holy Ark, facing the entrance to the synagogue. He cries aloud.*] "Hear, O Israel: the Lord our God, the Lord is one. Blessed be His name, whose glorious Kingdom is forever and forever." [*Stands as if rooted to the spot.*]

THE BEGGAR WOMAN [*jumps up with a weird cry. She begins to tremble, wailing frightfully and gazing about wildly. Suddenly she rushes forth from the synagogue with a piercing shriek.— The noise outside is at its height; sounds of rioting and pistol-shots*].

REB MAYSHE [*with glassy eyes*]. You took her away from here. You heard my prayer. Now I know that your army will come. Your miracle will happen, O Lord, dear God!

VOICES [*just outside the door*]. This way! This way! The door is open!

REB MAYSHE [*gives a sudden start, so that the crowbar falls from his hands. He strides forward with awe-in-*

spiring happiness]. They come! They come! "Who is like unto Thee, O Lord!"

LEON [*with a revolver in his hand, rushes in, calling to those behind him*]. He is here! He is here! [*Several young men hasten in.*]

REB MAYSHE [*disillusioned*]. What? They are coming to me? . . . No. . . . Not for . . . [*He falls dead.*]

LEON [*runs to him in fright*]. Grandpa! [*Falling before the corpse.*] Dead! [*Looks for a while at the body, and is lost in thought.*] Dead. The old order has departed. And . . . now . . . ?

CURTAIN

THE DUMB MESSIAH
A DRAMA IN THREE ACTS
[1911]

PERSONS OF THE DRAMA

MENAHEM PENINI, *Court Physician and Tax-Officer.*
RACHEL, *his daughter.*
AVIGDOR DE CORBEILLE.
LEAH, *his wife.*
HILLEL, *his son.*
REB JOSEPH, *Rabbi and Judge.*
REB SAMUEL SOSSEN.
REB JEHIEL.
THE BLIND MAN.
THE BLIND MAN'S SON.
THE BLIND MAN'S DAUGHTER-IN-LAW.
LEVI.
MIRIAM, *his wife.*
MESHULEM.
THE BEGGAR.
BLANCHE, *a prostitute.*
COUNT DE GUESCLIN.
FIRST SOLDIER.
SECOND SOLDIER.
A TRUMPETER.
MEN, WOMEN AND CHILDREN.

The action takes place in the year 1306, during the time of a great expulsion of the Jews from Illyria.

ACT I

A wide square before the gates of the city. To the right, the city wall with a deep gate-way. To the left, the road. In the background, the blue of the lofty mountains melts into the distant horizon. Two soldiers, armed with halberds, stand guard before the closed gate. They are listening to the confused murmur of voices behind the gate.

FIRST SOLDIER. Do you hear anything? They ought to be here by now. When the sun is high over the city, they must leave the land forever. Do you hear them coming?

SECOND SOLDIER. I hear a babble of voices,— the sounds of crying hard by the gate and further off. And far in the distance there's a noise of whistling and jeering. They're marching them out of the town.

FIRST SOLDIER. I went bathing yesterday and my ears are still full of water. You say they're crying?

SECOND SOLDIER. Ha-ha! . . . Such a moaning and wailing!

FIRST SOLDIER. The damned Jews! My cursed luck to be deaf on just this day, and not be able to hear their crying. It would sound sweeter to me than the dance music at the widow's tavern. But I'll join you in the laugh, just the same. Ha-ha-ha! Let them weep! Let them make up for the tears our Savior shed on His cross. Let them weep! [*Mocks the weeping.*] Oh, oy, ow!

Damned Christ-killers! Your time has come at last! . . . They thought God had forgotten them altogether, and they settled down in our city and land as if they were in their father's vineyard. No!! No rest for such as you! Out with you! Out into the wide world wherever your feet can carry you! Usurers, bloodsuckers, child-murderers! Christ-killers! God bless our wise king. He's driven the whole pack of them —

SECOND SOLDIER. Sh! . . . There are cries of suffering, too.

FIRST SOLDIER. Ha-ha-ha! Suffering? Fine! All the better! Cries of suffering! Ha-ha! It hurts 'em, does it? What a wise and good king is ours! He knew how to rub it in, all right. But it's a shame, I say, that he ordered them not to be harmed. Imagine! We must even protect them!

SECOND SOLDIER. Hm! That's something that vexes me to the very marrow. I'd like to take 'em, every man, woman and child of 'em, all sizes and ages, and crack their skulls for them, and kick them to Kingdom Come.

FIRST SOLDIER [*listening to the commotion inside the gate, and making thrusts in the air at imaginary enemies*]. I, too! I, too! Biff! Slam! One, two, and three! . . . It makes me sore to think that they put me on guard at this side of the gate. My! Wouldn't I like to be there looking over their bundles and having a hand in the inspection, to see whether they were carrying off any gold and silver, or jewels. My pockets are just crying for everything they own. . . .

SECOND SOLDIER. I guess the king's taken everything worth having from the cursed troop.

FIRST SOLDIER. Just the same I'd be satisfied to get what they've hidden on themselves. My empty pockets would —

SECOND SOLDIER. Hush! They're going to open the gate in a minute.

FIRST SOLDIER [*stretching himself full height against the wall, towards the inside*]. Won't somebody hold my hands back and bind my feet? I must be stronger than iron to resist the temptation to get at them.

SECOND SOLDIER. We'll each have to hold the other back. My hands itch so for their necks that I could scratch them to the bone without feeling the least pain. Ah! They're opening the gate! [*The gate opens from the inside, and there pour forth bent figures, men and women of all ages, carrying upon their backs bundles of various sizes. Groups of two and three are seen bearing small chests. Some of the women have children in their arms, while the older of the children are also carrying small bundles. All, except children under twelve, wear round saffron-yellow patches upon their breasts and backs. Women and children are wailing loudly. The men are deeply moved, dejected; many of them cannot restrain their tears.*]

FIRST SOLDIER [*greeting the expelled Jews with an outcry*]. Ha-a-a! Damned Jews! [*Swings his halberd about.*]

SECOND SOLDIER. Kr-r-r! Bah! [*The Jews look about them in terror, stoop even lower and proceed on their way. Some of them steal a sorrowful look back at the city, pause a moment, heave a deep sigh, look up to heaven and then, reluctantly, follow the others.— A* BLIND MAN *comes slowly through the gate, led by his son. The latter, with the other hand, supports his young, weeping wife, who is with child. All three bear packs upon their shoulders.*]

THE BLIND MAN [*as if continuing a conversation*]. The Messiah must come! I tell you, he must come!

The Blind Man's Daughter-in-Law [*through her tears*]. But where is he? Where is he?

The Blind Man. He must come! [*There is a sighing among the men, and a murmuring of " Yes, Yes." The women begin to weep all the louder at his words. Through the gate now comes* Levi, *a young man, with a tombstone upon his shoulder.* Miriam, *his wife, follows close by, carrying a bundle. At sight of* Levi *carrying the tombstone the two soldiers burst into a fit of uproarious laughter.*]

First Soldier. He's taking a tombstone along with him! . . . There goes a corpse with his headstone!

Second Soldier. He surely must think that he can cut it up into precious jewels.

Levi. On the grave from which I removed this stone, which is the holiest thing left in this life for me, you will find everything I own. Go, seek it there; you're welcome to it. [*Walks on, and mutters between his teeth.*] Take it, and may it choke you! [Reb Samuel Sossen *and* Reb Jehiel, *old men with bundles on their shoulders and staffs in their hands, come through the gate.*]

Sossen. Let us stop here! Call a halt! Let's wait until we've all come together.

Meshulem [*bearing a chest upon his back*]. Will we have to wait long? Are there many more yet?

Sossen. We'll soon see. Is it so hard for you to wait? Put down your chest and rest yourself.

Meshulem. And then have to lift it on my shoulders again? I can't get away from here quickly enough. Why should I pierce my eyes with the sight of our forbidden paradise?

Sossen. And how will you still the piercing grief in your heart, my dear Meshulem? Do be patient.

MIRIAM. Ah! It were best for me to drop dead where I stand!

JEHIEL. Many of us would gladly embrace the same fate. Perhaps all. But life and death are in God's hands. Why, look at me. I, aged as I am, must drag along with the rest into exile, with staff and wallet. I am eighty-three. Is it not high time that I should be in my grave, in eternal rest? But you see, I have not yet been called. It is God's will. Patience, my child. And faith. Everything will come in God's own way.

SOSSEN [*to the crowd*]. There is no need of your standing. You may sit down. We're allowed to wait here for the others. [*Amidst much weeping and sobbing, the exiles sit down upon the ground.*]

MIRIAM. And to think that the sun can still shine! How can it look down upon a scene like this?

FIRST SOLDIER. What do you call this? They're making a regular camp out of the place. Are we going to allow it?

SECOND SOLDIER. We ought to disperse them. I'll go in and ask the captain. [*Disappears within the gate. Some of the crowd approach and try to get another glimpse of the city.*]

FIRST SOLDIER. Off with you! Not a step nearer! Your infidel eyes are not to stain our holy Christian city with another glance! Bah! Away with you, dogs! I'll knock your eyes out for you, and chop your feet off. Brr! Lepers! [*The crowd retreats reluctantly, dejected and dispirited. One of them covers his face with his hands.*]

SECOND SOLDIER [*comes stamping through the gate.*] This is outrageous! Our orders are not to interfere with them!

FIRST SOLDIER. What! Then I throw up this job on

the instant. I'd sooner scratch my eyes out than stand here looking upon such a troop of unbaptized Christ-killers. [*Spits upon the Jews.*] Tfu! Tfu! [*Hurries through the gateway.*]

SECOND SOLDIER. I'm with you, there. Let our commander send whomever he pleases. But I don't stay here another moment. [*Spits at the Jews.*] Tfu! Tfu! [*Hurries after the other soldier.*]

LEVI. And we must suffer all this in patience! God in heaven!

SOSSEN. And is this new to you? How many summers have you been in the world? How long have you been a Jew? [*Several young men crawl cautiously nearer the gate and lie looking, full of longing, towards the city. Their faces are pale, their eyes wet with tears. A few can no longer restrain themselves, and bow their faces to the earth, weeping convulsively.*]

THE BLIND MAN. Word by word the forecasts of our holy prophets are coming true. The time is ripe for the Messiah. For such is the sign of our redemption: Before the Messiah comes, our Exile will become more bitter than ever. Can our Exile know greater bitterness than we now suffer? Are we not the most despised among peoples? They have despoiled us of all our wealth; we are poverty-stricken and wretched. David's son must come, even now.

DAUGHTER-IN-LAW. But he does not come! And what will become of me? I'll have to remain behind. My child may be born any day.

THE BLIND MAN'S SON. We begged them to let us stay till after the child was born, or at least not to deprive us of our horse and wagon. But they who preach the religion of brotherly love have hearts far harder than stone.

SOSSEN. Religion of brotherly love! Ah, young man, what things I could tell you— But here comes the Rabbi. [*Enter* REB JOSEPH, *a white-haired, bent old man, carrying under his arm a Holy Scroll, and on his shoulder a bundle. As he comes through the gate the sobbing and weeping grow louder.*]

REB JOSEPH [*in a feeble voice*]. Weep not, my faithful children, weep not. You need much strength for your journey, and tears will sap what little you have. And the way is far and long. . . .

MESHULEM. And whither does it lead?

MIRIAM. We ought every one of us march in a body to the sea and cast ourselves into its bosom.

REB JOSEPH. And is that our faith in God?

MESHULEM. What faith can a blighting hand inspire?

REB JOSEPH. My son, you sin to speak so. And why, despite everything, have you remained faithful to that blighting hand?

MESHULEM [*shaking his fists towards heaven*]. It is maddening. [*The lamentations break out anew.*]

REB JOSEPH. Sh-sh! Quiet!

MESHULEM. No! No! I'll bear it no longer! [*He jumps up and dashes through the gate back to the city.*]

SOSSEN. Meshulem, Meshulem! Turn back!— Woe to him, he has run to embrace the faith of our persecutors! [*All eyes are turned in terror towards the gate.* REB JOSEPH *rushes after the runaway, but comes to a halt at the gate, breathless. He leans heavily against the wall, his head bowed in grief.*]

THE BLIND MAN. Desertion of the faith is another token of our Redemption. For before the Messiah comes the weak and the wavering ones will fall away from their people and adopt the faith of our enemies. All the signs are here. The Messiah must come, I say. The time is ripe, and he will surely come.

THE BLIND MAN'S SON. But the sorrows that announce his coming, father, oppress us so mercilessly, that when the Messiah finally does arrive there will be none of us left to redeem. [*The sobbing breaks out anew.*]

REB JOSEPH [*turns back from the gate and addresses the people in as loud a voice as his strength can muster*]. Weep not! Let not your crying make the weak still weaker. Don't cry, I beg you. . . . For you sin against God with all this sobbing! It is true that you leave behind your nation and your homes, but you take with you your faith, which is eternal! Arise in all your pride! Make merry! See, have we not with us here the Sacred Scroll of the Law? Rejoice that you have remained faithful to our God! For you are martyrs, martyrs every one of you, and martyrs do not weep. You are all heroes, heroes in God's cause, and heroes do not weep! You have fought in battle, the greatest of all battles. A battle against yourselves, against your evil spirit. Naturally you were tempted to remain here. At the mere price of forsaking your faith you might have dwelt free and undisturbed in this nation, which for generations we have called our fatherland. But you triumphed over the evil spirit, in this most terrible of all battles, and carried off victory like true conquerors. Do conquerors weep at their triumphs? Do heroes return from their victories in tears? No! They chant joyous pæans and play merry music, clang the cymbals and dance to the sound of fife and drum. Weep not, women! Are you not all the sisters of Miriam, of Deborah, of Hannah? And you, my little children, stop your crying. For are you not like the seven sons of Hannah, who sacrificed themselves for the glory of God? Don't you know any songs at all? Have you already forgotten how to make merry? How does that little song run in which you praise the Lord for his eternal goodness? [*He begins to sing.*]

>Grievous woes our folk has borne
>Through its many generations

SOSSEN [*takes from his pocket a flute, and plays the melody*].

SOME OF THE CHILDREN AND WOMEN [*catch up the verses in mournful, broken voices*].

>In deepest trials, like manna,
>Help came sudden from above.
>Praise ye, then, our Father's mercy,
>For eternal is His love!
>Praise Him, thank Him . . .

>[*Enter* AVIGDOR DE CORBEILLE, *leading his wife* LEAH. *They are accompanied by several men, who are carrying many bundles.* LEAH *walks with fixed gaze, rarely looking at the people about her. Soon after comes* HILLEL, *son of* AVIGDOR, *walking backwards, one hand against the wall, the other upon his forehead. He mutters between teeth clenched in agony.*]

HILLEL. Illyria! Illyria! Mother-city! Fatherland! [*Suddenly he turns sharply around, and cries out in intense indignation.*] What?! You're singing here?! You're making music! [*He casts a look of anger and scorn upon the people.*]

AVIGDOR. What's the meaning of all this gayety?

SOSSEN. It's an antidote for dejection and discouragement.

HILLEL. And plunges us all the deeper into despair.

Weep, if you feel grief. [*He turns back to the gate and stands as if entranced.*]

REB JOSEPH. But we should feel *no* grief! We *must* not feel grief.

AVIGDOR. We should and must feel no sorrow. I know what you mean. But after all, those are mere words and are of no avail. [*Helps* LEAH *to a seat.*] Are we all here now?

SOSSEN. They're not closing the gates yet.

AVIGDOR. Oh, now I remember that I saw Penini's daughter hurrying along.

REB JOSEPH. Without her father? They've put him to death, then! God's will be done! [*A murmuring among the people. " Penini is dead! " . . . " They've killed Reb Menahem! " Sighing; an outburst of lamentation.*]

ONE OF THE MEN NEAR THE GATE. Here comes Penini's daughter now!

[*Enter* RACHEL, *a heavy pack on her shoulders. She is accompanied by two young girls, also carrying bundles, and several men, similarly burdened.* REB JOSEPH *and* SOSSEN *hurry to* RACHEL. HILLEL *steps out of her way, scarcely noticing her.* AVIGDOR *sits down beside* LEAH, *and buries his face in his hands.*]

REB JOSEPH. Where is your father?

RACHEL [*stretching out her arms to him, imploringly*]. Yes, where *is* my father? [*Her head sinks down upon her bosom.*]

SOSSEN. You've had no word from him at all?

RACHEL [*shakes her head*]. Not a word. Since that terrible day on which all the Jews of Illyria were arrested to have the royal decree of expulsion read to them, I have not seen him. That was a month ago. They set everybody free, except him. And what's happened to him I've been unable to find out.

REB JOSEPH. Neither have I. Every door and every mouth was closed tight.

RACHEL. There's only one explanation, then. I know that they've put him to death. I could read it in their eyes. They told me that they didn't know, but they couldn't look me in the face as they spoke. Oh, they must have tortured him horribly! For they treated me with such sympathy, and were so nice and kind to me. They even tried to persuade me to remain in the city. Where would I go, they asked me, bereft of my father and all my belongings? I thanked them and answered them freely. Without reserve I told them what I thought of their faith. It is a miracle that, as a token of their universal love, they did not burn me at the stake for it. . . . But who is crying here? And what are they crying for? The Lord has tried us in a crucible of fire, but we have all stood the test. The Exile is a great sieve through which he sifts out the dross among us. Is this, then, a cause for tears?

HILLEL. How hard!

RACHEL. No, young de Corbeille, I am not hard. I am firm, and such firmness we all need in this trying moment.

HILLEL. Leave us, at least, the consolation of our tears. We are saying farewell to our motherland forever. Do you feel no grief at all, at parting from your home?

RACHEL. My one grief is my father. Illyria is my stepmotherland, and I leave it with no regrets.

MIRIAM. And the graveyard? And the grave of your mother?

RACHEL [*shakes her head*]. No. Unlike the rest of

you, I did not lie for three days on the gravestones, filling the graves with my tears. This very morning I sought out my mother's grave, and my farewell was a brief one. "Mother," I said, "they deprive me of the hope of some day being buried where you sleep. But wheresoever I may die, our souls will meet at the throne of the same God. And although I shall never again behold your resting-place, you will live forever in my memory." I wept long and bitterly, I'll confess, but I knew that they were tears of weakness.

MIRIAM. You speak so because you have left behind in the graveyard only your mother. But if it had been a child of yours, a child you loved better than life itself. . . . Ah! It was only by force that they could tear me away from his little grave, and it was as if my darling child had died a second time. [*She falls upon the tombstone, sobbing convulsively.*]

A WOMAN. And how about my case?!

HILLEL. Do you see my mother? Her wandering mind, her strange look, her awful silence —

RACHEL [*seeing* LEAH *for the first time, utters a horrified exclamation*]. Poor woman!

HILLEL. She's been that way ever since they tore her away from the graves of her five children.

RACHEL. Poor, poor woman! She was not strong. At the gate to the cemetery I stopped for one last look. And suddenly a light dawned upon me. I raised my eyes to heaven, and cried out, "Lord, behold, we leave behind us here our dead, and the decayed branches of our people. Art thou content?"

REB JOSEPH. You're the daughter of your father; one can hear it in every word you utter. It is your father's spirit that speaks through you. Speak more, daughter of Penini, and strengthen the hearts of the discouraged.

HILLEL. I could almost believe that she is happy at the decree of exile, since it gives her opportunity to make a show of her strength — of her firmness, as she chooses to call it.

RACHEL. That's a malicious insult. His father is my father's enemy, and that explains his words.

AVIGDOR. Forgive him. It is his great sorrow that vents itself so. This whole night he was awake, wandering through every street in the city, so that he might bid farewell to every nook and corner.

HILLEL. My spirit is ill, my thoughts at a standstill; it seems that everything within me has died. Oh, my beloved home, my native city, my fatherland! [*Presses his hands to his head.*]

RACHEL. Where is that rock-like firmness for which we beseech the Lord in our daily prayers?

HILLEL. Yes, we pray for the power to remain steadfast to our God and our faith. And all of us have that power, even those who lie here weeping. Even I, whose heart is torn with grief. But as to the power not to weep, not to cry out when misfortune so assails us — no, such power I do not ask. For it is cruelty, inhumanity. You see, I am not crying, either. I am man enough to restrain my tears. But I understand those who weep, and even envy them the tears they shed so freely. Nor do I pour vinegar into their wounds by asking, "Who's crying here?" . . . "What are they all weeping about?"

RACHEL [*through her clenched teeth*]. They killed my father! Do you understand?

HILLEL [*looks at her for a moment, his eyes distended, then lowers his head*].

BLANCHE [*comes through the gate, sobbing loudly. Her arms are covered with little bundles. She is a buxom woman, in her forties*]. How they rummaged through every bundle of mine! With what curse can I curse such as they?

THE BEGGAR [*comes in behind* BLANCHE. *He is a man of about forty, in tatters, with staff and empty wallet*]. They kept me a long time, too. They refused to believe that I was so poor. I must look like a rich man in disguise.

BLANCHE [*putting down her bundles, and making some of them firmer, all the while weeping*]. The officer recognized me. "Blanche," he advised me, "better get baptized and stay behind with us. Why should you lose everything?"— And I said to him, "I may lose everything, but not my God!" I have sinned enough, without deserting my faith. [*Suddenly breaks out into hysterical crying.*] My sins have brought this upon you! My sins! [*Beats her breasts with clenched fists.*] Burn me! Stone me! My sins have brought all this upon you! [*Takes the end of a cord into her mouth, and busies herself tying a bundle.*]

THE BEGGAR. And here they sit. What are we waiting for?

SOSSEN. And why are you so impatient?

THE BEGGAR. At the start I like to know the end, and if we must be off, what's the good of sitting?

THE BLIND MAN'S SON. Yes, really. Why are we still lying about here?

SOSSEN. They have not yet closed the gates against us.

LEVI. And then, too, do we know yet whither we are going?

SOSSEN. We are going to the first land that will open its gates to us. And there shall we remain.

THE BEGGAR. My idea exactly.

REB JOSEPH. I have had enough of Christian nations. I have suffered enough humiliation,— have been forced to listen to sermons urging our people to desert their faith, preached by bloodthirsty priests in my own synagogue. I have been presented with a yellow patch. . . . [*Looks with loathing at the yellow patch on his breast, and shakes his head.*] I have watched them burn our holy books, so that for years I have not had a Talmud to look into. Ah — ah! . . . And more than one blood accusation I have suffered through. . . . Yes, yes. Enough of the Christian lands, enough! . . . The idea of leaving them has been for a long time upon my mind. Better far to dwell among Mohammedans, or even with idol-worshippers. But something always held me back. It was so hard for me to leave you. And now I am too old, and want a little rest and peace. For once, at least, I want to prepare for the celebration of our sacred Passover without the fear that the humane Christians will stain our Passover-cakes with *our* blood, and then say that we have used the blood of Christians in kneading them. I long for Africa, for Egypt, and if God is good, He will bring me to the Land of Israel, the land of all lands, the goal of all goals.

REB JEHIEL. In my opinion we ought merely to cross the border and wait there. Mark my words, they'll call us back before long.

BLANCHE. Oh, God grant it! I'll not move a step from the boundary line.

FIRST MAN. It's Spain for me. Reb Samuel is the present tax-officer of Toledo. And if you took my advice, we'd all go there.

SECOND MAN. Italy, too, is a safe place for Jews these days.

THIRD MAN. And what about Germany? Emperor

Albrecht is favorable to us. That's where *I'll* go. I have a first cousin living at Frankfurt.

RACHEL [*she has been listening to the conversation with a bitter smile, and shakes her head sadly*]. We Jews want to disperse to the four corners of the earth and thus add to the miseries of our Exile. [*Her words attract the immediate attention of all, and they raise their eyes to her.*] Each one seeks a spot for himself, and our whole people remains without a home. [*The interest of the people grows.* HILLEL *looks at her out of the corner of his eye. Others draw nearer to* RACHEL.] You would build new homes, and have forgotten the old one. [REB JOSEPH *sobs.*]

SOSSEN. The old home?

RACHEL. Yes, the land of all lands, the goal of all goals.

AVIGDOR [*with an impatient gesture*] You mean —?

SOSSEN and OTHERS. The Holy Land?

RACHEL. The Holy Land.

SOSSEN. But the Holy Land is too distant, my daughter. I favor frequent halts. You remember how it is written? "And they wandered forth, and then they rested." Well, such is our destiny. One continuous journeying, resting and journeying forth again.

THE BEGGAR. That's just my way of doing.

RACHEL. A beggar's way the destiny of Israel?

SOSSEN. Is this the first time you hear it, proud daughter? [*Ironic laughter and sighing from the crowd.*] Long, long indeed have we wandered whither our eyes have taken us, whither the winds have blown us. Like beggars we knock at doors, our heads bowed, our backs cringing, and kiss, in all submission, the hand that deigns to open a door to us. Now our way points to the South. And southward we shall go, and stop at the first door. The Holy Land is far, far away, my dear daughter. Our people will not have the persistence to travel so far.

RACHEL. And what if all the doors that lie near are closed against us?

SOSSEN [*sweeping her objection aside with a gesture*]. Yes, yes, but they are *not* closed. There are Italy, Spain, Germany. . . .

RACHEL. There you are! So we Jews do want to be dispersed, after all. And of all the sins of Israel, that is the greatest. Our prayers are full of Zion, but we do not mean what we pray. How then can God take our prayers in earnest?

REB JOSEPH. Daughter, don't talk like that. We have been punished severely enough. Don't make us out to be greater sinners than we are. Our hearts *are* in our prayers. We beseech the Lord, and await His pleasure.

RACHEL. No, Israel's heart is numbed, and no longer does he understand God's sign.

SOSSEN. What sign?

RACHEL. Our Exile. . . . This expulsion from our age-long homes.

THE BLIND MAN. The Messiah speaks through the girl's lips!

AVIGDOR. The Holy Land! The place is a desert, the cities are in ruins, the soil is barren. What shall we do there? Poverty-stricken, robbed of all we own, without a single day's provisions. [*Sighs and sobs from the people.*] What shall we be able to do in the desert? Where shall we get food, and who will there be to help us?

THE BEGGAR. My whole business is threatened! I refuse to go there!

Rachel. I speak of a land that we have never ceased to love,— the only place where we can truly feel at home.

Hillel. Ah, nowhere shall I feel at home. For *my* home was Illyria. Henceforth I am an exile; from this moment I become a homeless wanderer. [*The sighing and sobbing breaks forth anew.*] Wherever I shall be, my heart will long for Illyria. How dear to me is every spot, every blade of grass, every bush and tree! How glorious its skies, how precious every breath of its air! Ah! One loves only his native spot, the place where his cradle was rocked.

Rachel [*shaking her head sadly*]. You all know my father. [*Her voice begins to quiver.*] That is, you all *knew* him. He was born in Illyria, and was deeply devoted to it. He was always among its most loyal sons. More than once he gave proof of his love for Illyria, as tax-officer and as court-physician, and to him no sacrifice was too great for his native land. Yet still greater than this love was his love for the Old Home; his deepest longing was the Holy Land. This was his inspiration, and it gave to him even the wings of a poet. Let me recite for you a hymn, written by my father long ago, in which he pours out the innermost feelings of his heart. I know he would have chanted it far better than I. [*Her voice falters.*] He would most surely have lifted your hearts in mighty, throbbing exaltation, just as he moved my own. But — [*She struggles with her emotion.*] His mouth, that spoke golden words . . . is . . . silenced . . . forever. [*She bursts into tears. Several women are overcome by her sorrow, and weep with her.* Rachel *recovers her self-control, and begins to recite the psalm, at first in a soft voice, choked with tears, gradually rising to a note of deep yearning and pathos.*]

What makes my heart so tender, and brings such painful
   throbbing?
The pain is from my yearning; my yearning, from my
   love.
What chokes my throat with tear-drops,— hot tears that
   scald my eyelids?
The tears flow from my yearning; my yearning, from my
   love.
There lies a Land far eastward,— a City, where God
   once dwelt.
I need but to recall it, and grief brims o'er my heart;
The yearning longs for utterance, and I dissolve in tears.
I behold it in all its splendor, peopled by happy throngs,
I see in all its glory, the City that David ruled.
I do not know the Land, yet is my love for it unbounded;
I have never looked upon it, yet it fills my sight, my
   heart.
I hear its sacred name pronounced and straight my heart
   is moved;
Whether awake or in my sleep, it is my soul's one dream.
How I yearn for thee, Jerusalem! City where our
   prophets preached.
How I long for thee, Land chosen by God Himself for us.
Let Him but lead me to thee, I will fall on my knees
   and kiss thy ground,
As never yet a lover showered his beloved with kisses.
My tears of joy will fructify thy soil,
My jubilant cries will thunder through thy breezes.
Who shall lead me to thy breast, there to nestle like a
   child against its mother!
Oh, my heart is breaking, my soul is stifled with a yearn-
   ing
That grows from day to day together with my years.
Zion, my beloved! Jerusalem! Dearest of sweethearts!

[*She stops, lost in abstraction, her tearful eyes gazing far off into the distance. The hearers are plainly stirred and remain rooted to their places. A soft weeping.*]

AVIGDOR [*half to himself*]. Ah, well! 'Tis but a song.

RACHEL [*slowly lowering her glance to* AVIGDOR]. And is that all Avigdor de Corbeille has to say? Has every longing for our ancient home really died within him?

REB JOSEPH [*drying his eyes*]. Will you take counsel from me, your old Rabbi? Let us depart for the Land of Israel. All together.

THE BEGGAR. It's a bargain. There'll be houses there to get alms from, won't there?

BLANCHE. How long will it take us to get there?

SOSSEN. That's the important point.

REB JOSEPH. If we are determined to reach the Holy Land, what matters the length of the journey? We set ourselves a goal, and we will attain it.

RACHEL. That's the proper spirit, friends. Let us only *will* it, and the rest is easily accomplished. You have just displayed great heroism. You left your native country for the sake of our faith. Now show courage and achieve the land to which our faith is bound by eternal ties. My people, what do you say? Are you willing?

MANY VOICES. We are! We are!

RACHEL [*ecstatically*]. Then, forward at once! Under God's banner! [*The people arise and take up their bundles. Cries of:* " Forward! " . . . " Let's make a start." . . . " Let's be off, then."]

THE BLIND MAN [*in exaltation*]. The Messiah's spirit moves among us!

SOSSEN [*shouting*]. Hold! The gates are still open.

We must wait. There must be some Jews still on the way.

REB JEHIEL. Or perhaps . . .

SOSSEN. What other explanation can there be?

REB JEHIEL. Perhaps — with the Lord's aid all things are possible . . . perhaps they have reconsidered their action? Maybe God has turned the King's mind from evil to good, and we'll be invited to return. [*Commotion among the people; murmuring.*]

HILLEL [*as if suddenly awakening*]. God in Heaven! [*Raises his hands toward heaven.*]

RACHEL [*observing the crowd, with fright on her face*]. Almighty God!

REB JEHIEL. Help has always come to us in the hour of our greatest need. For only one night Ahasuerus did not sleep, yet the Jews were all saved.

SOSSEN. What a great miracle that would be!

AVIGDOR. But it will not happen. The king needs our money. And his coffers are mightier than his heart.

REB JEHIEL. But the hearts of kings and prinees are in God's hand.

BLANCHE. Oh, if God would only show us now his great mercy. . . . I am unworthy of it. [*Drags her bundles nearer to the gate.*]

THE BLIND MAN'S DAUGHTER-IN-LAW. Dear God, show us thy miracle!

MIRIAM. Thou hast the power, O Lord! The power is thine! [*The crowd begins to edge nearer to the gate; a troubled and excited conversation arises.*]

THE BLIND MAN. Impossible! The Messiah must come. It was forecast in the writings of the holy scholar Reb Simon, son of Johai, in his sacred work called the "Zohar." When the sixtieth, or six-and-sixtieth year will have crossed the threshold of the sixth millennium of the world, then the Messiah will arrive. We are now in the six-and-sixtieth year. . . . The time is ripe for the Messiah. But before he appears, our sorrows will grow more in number, not less.

SossEN. I place my trust sooner in God's wonders than in the calculations of a Cabbalist.

MIRIAM. Oh, dear God! Father in heaven! [*The babble of voices breaks out once more, followed by a sudden silence. The two soldiers come through the gate, escorting a man bound with ropes. They thrust him to the ground and return, stopping at the gate.*]

FIRST SOLDIER. We're closing the gates now against you forever, you Jews. Any one of you that makes his way back to this city will be either beheaded or forcibly baptized. Such is the decree of the King and the Holy Church! [*The soldiers disappear. The gates swing heavily to. A loud wailing breaks out. HILLEL hides his face in his hands, his bosom heaving.*]

RACHEL. My father! My father! [*Covers her face and sobs.*]

AVIGDOR [*ironically*]. There is your miracle! I knew it!

THE BLIND MAN. The Messiah is near.

REB JOSEPH. Who is it that the soldiers brought? [*With* SossEN *and several others he approaches the bound figure.*] Penini! Reb Menahem! Blessed be He who bringeth the dead back to life!

RACHEL [*with an outcry*]. My father! [*She rushes to the bound figure, followed by her companions. The crowd makes way for her. She approaches the newcomer, whom* REB JOSEPH *and* SossEN *have by this time released from his ropes and are supporting under the arms. She throws herself upon his neck with hysterical tears and laughter.*] Father! You live! You live! [*She kisses his face and hands in wild joy.*] I thought that they had put you to death! . . . Oh, how I burned with grief because I did not know where you had disappeared! . . . I clenched my teeth so as not to go insane with the agony! . . . Father! My father!

PENINI [*his eyes filled with tears, kisses his daughter, fondles her cheeks affectionately, holds her away from him so that he may get a good look at her, then presses her close to him again and kisses her. Strange tones of deep, repressed sighs force their way through his lips. He embraces her tenderly, now kissing one cheek, now the other, gradually making his way with her to the foreground. The crowd, deeply moved, makes way for them.* RACHEL's *companions follow, and kiss the folds of* PENINI's *cloak*].

RACHEL. Father! Father!— Oh, let me look at you!— How gray you've become! They tortured you!— Your face is bruised!— And they've plucked your beard. [*With a sudden scream of horror.*] Oh! Your nails! . . .

PENINI [*caresses her, and seeks to calm her*].

RACHEL. How you must have suffered! What agony! Oh, father, father, father dear!

PENINI [*breathes with difficulty, and bites his lips as if to restrain a violent fit of weeping*].

RACHEL. Speak! Tell us all about it.

PENINI [*from his tightly compressed lips he utters a strange cry of grief, and covers his face*].

RACHEL [*clasping his hands*]. Father! What is the trouble? Father!

SOSSEN. He must have undergone terrible things at

their hands. I've had a taste of it myself. [*Sobbing and sighing among the people. Cries of " Yes! " " Yes! "*]

Miriam. He hasn't yet uttered a single word! That's how horribly they tortured him.

Penini [*repeats his strange cry of grief*].

Rachel. Father! My darling father! Speak! Let me hear your voice again, if only for a single word! Speak out, cry out your sufferings, your humiliation. . . . Father!

Penini [*suddenly draws to his full height, opens his mouth wide, and, clinging to* Rachel, *cries in pitiful tones*]. — augh — er! [Daughter.] [*The crowd is seized with horror. People recoil from* Penini *in fright.*]

Rachel [*shudders, her hands on her cheeks, then looks upon her father with eyes distended in consternation*].

Penini [*his voice is somewhat stronger, but more tearful than before. He points to his mouth*]. — augh — er! [*Bursts into tears. A commotion among the people. There is a frightened murmuring:* " *His tongue.*" . . . " *His tongue.*"]

Rachel [*screaming in horror*]. His tongue! They've cut out his tongue! [*She swoons.* Hillel *catches her and lays her tenderly down. Her companions hasten to her assistance and revive her. When she comes to, she breaks into a hysteric wailing.* Reb Joseph, Sossen, Avigdor, Reb Jehiel *and others gather about* Penini *in great terror.*]

Leah [*arises slowly, looks at* Rachel, *then at* Penini, *from whom she does not remove her eyes.*]

Penini [*ceases his weeping, dries his cheeks, opens his eyes, gazes about him, then walks over to* Rachel *and lays his hand upon her*].

Act I] THE DUMB MESSIAH

RACHEL [*shuddering*]. Father! Father! [*Turns her face towards the ground and weeps.*]

PENINI. — augh — er. E — ough. — op — kh — yi-g. [Enough, stop crying.] [*She continues to weep.* PENINI *then makes signs to the people about him that he wants to write something.*]

HILLEL [*goes over to a small package, takes out a writing-tablet and a stylus and gives them to* PENINI].

PENINI [*writes down something, and thrusts the tablet before* RACHEL's *eyes*].

RACHEL [*shudders and utters a wild exclamation*].

PENINI [*gives the tablet to* HILLEL, *pointing to* RACHEL].

HILLEL [*deeply moved, reads to* RACHEL]. "Stop crying," writes your father. Calm yourself. Control yourself. For from this day on you must be his tongue.

PENINI [*nodding sadly, and speaking with difficulty*]. M-m-y — ongue! [My tongue.] [*He utters his syllables very slowly. His " n " is nasal, while the " g " and " r " are guttural, and the " f " is blown through the lips rather than pronounced.*]

RACHEL [*struggles to master her tears*].

PENINI [*surveys the crowd. His glance falls upon* AVIGDOR].

AVIGDOR [*hastens to* PENINI's *side with outstretched hand*]. We were enemies, Menahem Penini, and lived through all our days in enmity and envy. . . .

PENINI [*makes a gesture of protest*].

AVIGDOR. It makes no difference which of us envied the other. It makes no difference which of us was the guilty one. Now we are friends once more. Now everything is forgotten.

PENINI [*grasps* AVIGDOR's *hand in a hearty clasp*].

Sossen. Common sorrows bring reconciliation and peace.

The Beggar. Yes, when there's no further profit in continuing the quarrel.

Penini [*shakes his head, with a bitter smile*].

Reb Joseph [*as if suddenly recalling something, and seeking to brush the unwelcome thought aside, passes his hand over his face*]. Well, brothers and sisters, the gates have closed upon us forever. Then let us be off. There is nothing else for us to wait for. Say a last good-by to your native city, now, without tears, if you can, and with courage and pride. Remember the holy goal we have set ourselves. Peace be to you, Illyria! Our heartfelt gratitude to you for the joyous days we spent within your gates. And for the evil that we suffered you will have to give account to the Righteous Judge above. We were loyal to you and loved you with all our hearts. But you did not care for our love any longer. May God judge you, but with more love and mercy than you judged us. Peace be unto you! [*There is a general wailing, and the people shoulder their bundles.*]

Penini [*breathing heavily, with fixed gaze*].

Rachel [*arises and rushes to embrace him.*] Father!

Reb Joseph. Reb Menahem, just before you came, your daughter, filled with your spirit, won us over to the Land of Israel.

Penini [*in happy surprise*]. Go-k! [God].

Reb Joseph. Yes, she spoke to us just as you yourself would have done, and gladly we voted to make the journey to the Holy Land.

Penini [*in great joy he raises* Rachel's *head, looks at her with deepest love, and, with eyes turned to heaven, cries out in ecstasy*]. Go-k, m-my — ongue! [God! My tongue!]

Act I] THE DUMB MESSIAH 195

Reb Joseph. Yes, she is indeed your tongue. Be our leader, now, Penini. Lead us to the land of our longings, to our home of old.

Penini [*makes an emphatic nod of assent, his eyes still raised to heaven*]. Ye — [Yes]! [*He lowers his gaze, and it falls upon the Holy Scroll in* Reb Joseph's *arms. He embraces it impulsively, clasps it to his bosom, raises it in both his hands and stands exalted in silent prayer. There is a deep silence, as if none would desecrate the moment with noise.*]

Leah [*walks all around* Penini, *looking at him with an expression of puzzled awe*].

Penini [*turns to the crowd, holding the Holy Scroll aloft. With firm, slow steps he walks to the left*].

Rachel, *spreading out her arms, inspired*]. Forward! On our way! [*Turns to her bundle, and shoulders it. There is a bustle among the people. Quiet, repressed weeping.*] When the Jews came forth from Egypt it was with song upon their lips. From afar there beckoned to them a home all their own. That same home now beckons to us. No more tears! No more wailing! Sing, Jews; sing songs of praise to the Lord! Sing praise to the Lord!

SLOW CURTAIN

Which descends while Rachel is speaking.

ACT II

A camp on the seashore; in the background, the sea. From the left center stretches a road that reaches the middle of the stage, then turns around to the sea and leads to a high cliff which hides the water from view. To the right of the cliff grows a large tree. On both sides of the stage, tents; to the left, behind the foremost tent, a tree. From the water's edge come the sounds of splashing waves and children at play.

THE BEGGAR *goes about from one tent to the other, stopping at each entrance. He bows his head, stretches out his hand, takes it back as if he had been given something, shoves it into his wallet, nods thanks, and mumbles. At other times he makes a wry face, as if he had been refused alms, lowers his hand with a sigh, and walks off sulkily.*

BLANCHE [*running in from behind the hill*]. What are you doing at my tent? What are you looking for there?

THE BEGGAR. I'm merely practicing. Practicing, that's all. I don't want to forget the fine points of my trade.

BLANCHE. All my belongings are tied good and strong. You won't be able to steal a thing.

THE BEGGAR. I never steal. I simply beg. Don't you see how I bow my head? How is it that I can tell

by a look at you just how you earn your living? You
ought to do like me, and keep in practice lest you forget
your trade.

BLANCHE [*screaming*]. Listen, Jews, to his talk!
His mouth reeks with filth. Why didn't they cut out
his tongue?

THE BEGGAR. As for you, they should have drawn
and quartered you altogether.

BLANCHE. You low-down beggar, I'll grab hold of
you and throw you into the sea!

THE BEGGAR. Into the sea of your lust, you mean?
My word as a man, you won't do anything of the kind!

BLANCHE. Bah! [*She disappears into her tent*].

THE BEGGAR. Bah yourself! [*He stretches his hand
to the opening of* BLANCHE's *tent, derisively, and withdraws it at once. His face contracts in scornful disgust,
and he walks away. As he comes to the foremost tent
upon the left,* RACHEL *issues from it.*]

RACHEL. Do you want something?

THE BEGGAR. No, my noble damsel, I need nothing.
I'm merely practicing. [*He proceeds on his way, and
is soon lost among the tents*].

RACHEL [*remains standing in the entrance to her
tent, gazes out over the sea, and then towards the
opposite tent on the right. She walks slowly by it,
casting furtive glances inside. At last she comes to a
stop near the tree, still eyeing the tent restlessly, as if
she would not care to be discovered*].

HILLEL [*comes out of the tent she is watching*].

RACHEL [*blushes deeply, and is about to leave*].

HILLEL [*stopping her with his outstretched hand*].
Are you looking for some one? Tell me, and I'll call
him for you.

RACHEL. I have my companions.

HILLEL. Perhaps you are looking for them?

RACHEL. They're in their tent.

HILLEL. This is the sixth day that we've been together.

RACHEL. That's just how many I counted, too.

HILLEL. Rachel!

RACHEL. How is your mother feeling?

HILLEL. She is resting comfortably, thank you. But I wanted to say that —

RACHEL. Ah, how beautiful the sea is! I look and look upon it, and cannot turn my eyes away. Last night, when sleep would not come to me, I lay awake and listened to the rhythm of its waves. It sounded like heavenly music.

HILLEL. You do not care to hear me.

RACHEL. Did you say anything? It seems that only I am speaking, and that I could talk forever. Yonder, far over the waves lies the land of our dreams, the goal of our longing.

HILLEL [sadly]. In my dreams I see Illyria. And — you.

RACHEL [embarrassed]. Ha-ha. You'll not find me in Illyria. Your dream is false.

HILLEL. Yet I behold you in it. [A sound of laughter from the children at play.]

RACHEL. Just listen to the laughter of the children. To them it is as if God had created the vast sea as their own playground.

HILLEL. Rachel, I dreamed of you.

RACHEL. What? Oh, to be sure. Yes, so you were telling me. But why speak about dreams? Dreams are so silly. [The children laugh again.] They must be having a jolly time! I must run to them and watch their games.

HILLEL [*seizing her hand*]. Rachel!
RACHEL [*softly*]. Hillel, let me go.
HILLEL. Be frank.
RACHEL. Why — what do you mean?
HILLEL. You were but just now looking for me.
RACHEL. It was wrong of you to spy upon me from your tent.
HILLEL. Last night I was awakened by weeping — a bitter wailing, that plucked at my very heartstrings.
RACHEL. I heard nothing, though I scarcely closed my eyes.
HILLEL. Yes, you heard nothing then, and you don't wish to hear. It was my love weeping within me, like a strayed child looking for its home. So I lay all the night through, with eyes wide open, gazing across to your tent. All morning, too, I have been watching the same spot. I saw how you came to the opening of your tent this morning, and looked over to mine. And that same longing that I now know so well, was in *your* eyes, too. I jumped up with your name on my lips — but your father came out to you. What joy I felt, and how much greater and deeper than ever my yearning became, when I saw you look away from your father and steal another glance at me!
RACHEL. At you?
HILLEL. Well then, at my tent,— the opening of it.
RACHEL [*her eyes closed*]. No. At you! At you!
HILLEL [*with a cry of jubilation*]. Rachel! [*Embraces her and kisses her passionately. For a moment they stand as if entranced.*]
RACHEL [*suddenly coming to herself and trying to thrust him away*]. No! No!
HILLEL. My darling!
RACHEL No! No! Impossible!

Hillel. What do you mean? What is impossible?

Rachel. My father . . .

Hillel. Your father will not stand in the way of our happiness, nor will mine.

Rachel. But you do not know my father's plans.

Hillel. Plans? Has he any plans for you? Has he already chosen a husband for you? And is that man among us?

Rachel [*shakes her head*]. No, no. . . . It's something else . . . entirely different. . . .

Hillel. But what is it that can come between us and make our union impossible?

Rachel. That I cannot tell you. It is a secret. My father's greatest secret.

Hillel. Then — [*looking away*]. I'm the unluckiest of men. One misfortune after another. First my mother, then my home, and now . . .

Rachel. That's why I wanted to hide my feelings from you. But you made me confess!

Hillel [*passionately*]. But you *do* love me! You love me! Tell it to me! Let me hear you say it! I want to drink it in with every fiber of my being! Tell it to me! You love me! You love me!

Rachel [*closing her eyes*]. I — love — you!

Hillel [*jubilant*]. Oh! [*Falls on his knees before her, burying his face in the folds of her dress.*]

Rachel [*as before, placing her hand tenderly upon his head*]. I — love — you! [*From the water's edge there come running in a group of merry children. Laughing and shouting they cross to the road on the left and disappear. As they run by,* Rachel *shudders and opens her eyes.*]

Hillel. This is — the awakening. [*Rises slowly.*]

Rachel [*covers her face with both hands*].

HILLEL. If a man stands between a high cliff and the deep sea, what can be his end?

RACHEL [*closing her eyes once more, she shudders and stretches out a hand towards him*].

HILLEL. Such will be *my* end, between my love and your father's secret.

RACHEL. Hillel, your words stab me!

HILLEL [*passionately*]. And is there no hope left me at all? Tell me. I can hardly believe it. My father was supposed to go to Italy. You and I should have reached the parting of our ways on the second day after the expulsion. But suddenly my poor mother took it into her head to refuse to leave your father, and we were forced to remain with her. So that you and I did not separate after all, and with every day, with every hour, with every step, our heaven-sent love grows within us. For surely it was God's will that kept us together. And there is no other between us — is there? You said so yourself. Your father has not chosen any other for you?

RACHEL. No. [*Softly, and slowly.*] He wants me all for himself.

HILLEL. What? What can that mean? What sacrifices does he ask of you?

RACHEL. Listen, then. He — but first give me your oath. . . . No, you needn't swear. Whatever I tell you, you are to forget at once. I know that they could not tear it from you even by torture.

HILLEL. Your secret will be sacred to me, Rachel.

RACHEL [*looking about and lowering her voice*]. As soon as all of us who have been driven from Illyria are happily settled in the Holy Land, my father plans to journey through all the lands where the Jews dwell in their exile, and summon them back to their ancient home.

HILLEL [*not understanding her*]. Well? So what?

RACHEL. So I must go with him. He will be Moses, and I, his Aaron. He, the head and the masterly will; I, his tongue.

HILLEL. So that is it!

RACHEL. I must be free, and belong to him alone.

HILLEL. Your father wants to be the Messiah!

RACHEL. Whosoever will come to summon our people from their exile, and lead them forth from it,—he will be the Messiah, he will be our Savior.

HILLEL. That differs from my belief in the Messiah. Not any man at all can be our Savior. He must be sent by God, and come from the house of David.

RACHEL. How will you recognize him? Surely not at first, but only at the end, when our people shall have been delivered.

HILLEL. But the Messiah himself will know that he has been sent by God. The Lord will reveal it to him plainly enough.

RACHEL. In the darkness of the dungeon, wracked and tortured, in terrible agony; his tongue cut out because, in his grief at the decree of expulsion, he had dared to utter a harsh word against the king, my father beheld a vision.

HILLEL. Proclaiming him the —

RACHEL. He lay there waiting for death, which he felt was but a matter of hours. But his mind was only upon the horrible fate of his people, and his heart was breaking with despair. Suddenly it seemed to him that a voice was calling, a voice that spoke to him and said, "You shall not die. You shall go forth from this place and lead the Jews out of exile!" And he felt that his tongue had been restored to him.

HILLEL. But his tongue was not restored, Rachel.

RACHEL. Yet his life was spared and he was freed, and I was his tongue, and with *his* thoughts of Zion I won over our people.

HILLEL. Do *you* believe that your father is the Messiah?

RACHEL [*softly, after a brief silence*]. To me he is my father.

HILLEL. And that means —?

RACHEL. That I am his tongue, and so shall be forever. I'll read the tiniest thought from his eyes; his every breath will inspire me with the most fiery words. Wherever he goes, I will follow —

HILLEL. But our new found love, Rachel?

RACHEL [*she pretends that she has not heard, but her voice quivers*]. And all the children of exile will answer our call. They who have suffered persecution through the ages, who have been driven from place to place, will all rally to our banner. They who long for rest, who yearn for the ancient home, will follow us. From East and West, from North and South, joyous armies of Jews will march back to their home of old, the old love flaming up anew in their breasts, radiant with hope and gladness!

PENINI [*comes out of his tent. His face expresses great surprise and happiness*]. —augh—er! [Daughter.]

RACHEL [*hastening to him*]. Father!

PENINI [*takes her in his arms and clasps her tightly to his heart. He kisses and caresses her. Then, still holding her close to him, he casts a penetrating glance at* HILLEL].

HILLEL [*calmly, after a brief pause*]. Reb Menahem Penini, I love your daughter.

Penini [*shudders, then moans*]. Oh — oh! [*Turns to* Rachel, *raising her eyes to his. She lowers her eyes.*]

Hillel. She loves me, too. [Penini *gasps in fright.*]

Rachel. No, father, no! I'll stay with you. I'll be true to you. I love him ever so much — I haven't yet told him how deeply. But you are more to me than anything else in the world. More than my life. More than my love.

Penini [*tears his hair, groans, clenches his teeth, stamps his foot, beats his mouth in desperation, breathing with difficulty*].

Rachel [*throwing herself on her knees before him, seizing his hands*]. No, no, father! Father! Don't suffer so! It breaks my heart! [*In tears.*] I can't bear to see it. I can't bear to see it!

Penini [*gradually becoming calm, his eyes closed. Soon he opens them, and looks at* Rachel *and* Hillel. *He frees one hand and points first to* Hillel, *then to his daughter and himself.* Rachel *looks on, puzzled.* Penini *repeats his gestures with more emphasis*]. Ig — he — wig — ug? [Is he with us?]

Rachel [*catching his meaning*]. Whether he's with us, you ask?

Penini [*nodding*]. Ye — [Yes]. [Rachel *lowers her head.* Penini, *his bosom heaving with emotion, looks beseechingly at* Hillel, *and points to* Rachel.] —e ig my —ongue. [She is my tongue.]

Hillel. I'll not take her away from you, Reb Menahem. But don't you take her away from me, either. Give her to me. And your ways shall be my ways. Wherever you go, I will follow. And if I cannot speak for you, I will not keep her from being your tongue. [Penini *looks at him with an unwavering gaze.*]

Rachel [*raising her eyes slowly, in soft entreaty*].

Father!

PENINI [*still gazing at* HILLEL. *He breathes hard. Then he looks at* RACHEL. *Tears come to his eyes, and his features twitch. Tenderly he frees himself from* RACHEL, *turns around and walks off a few paces. For a moment he stops, raises his eyes to heaven, dries his tears, and takes from his bosom the writing-tablet. He writes down something, turns back and hands the tablet to* HILLEL *and* RACHEL, *who have watched him in pain and deepest sympathy*].

RACHEL [*in joyous surprise*]. The wedding will take place in the Holy Land! [*Throws her arms about her father's neck*]. Oh! Father! [PENINI *embraces her fondly, and kisses her on the forehead.*]

HILLEL. God bless you, Reb Menahem!

PENINI [*looks at* HILLEL *with the same unwavering glance as before, then offers him his hand.* HILLEL *grasps it eagerly and kisses it.* PENINI, *his eyes full of tears, which he attempts to hide by covering his face, turns away from* HILLEL *and* RACHEL *and goes back towards his tent*].

HILLEL [*with arms outspread*]. My Rachel!

RACHEL [*falling into his arms*]. My Hillel! [*They kiss passionately.— Suddenly there arises a great commotion to the left. . . . There is a scurrying hither and thither, and a babble of many voices.*]

VOICES [*shouting*]. A messenger is hurrying to us! A messenger! [*From far off comes the sound of glad cries. "Hurrah! Hurrah! Good news! Joy! Joy!"*]

PENINI [*at the entrance to his tent. Shudders, then steps into the road and looks with wide open eyes in the direction of the popular tumult*].

HILLEL [*softly, as if intoxicated*]. Do you hear?

They're shouting Joy! Yes, joy! Joy and happiness!

RACHEL. My darling! My only one!

HILLEL. Never before have I heard your voice so sweet and so tender. Sweetheart! [*They kiss.— The shouts grow louder, and have come nearer.*]

VOICES. It's Meshulem! — it's Meshulem! — Meshulem's come with good news!

AVIGDOR [*rushes out of his tent and takes the road to the left.* REB JEHIEL, SOSSEN, BLANCHE *and others come running in from the right. Enter* MESHULEM, *in rider's costume, surrounded by a throng of men, women and children.* HILLEL *and* RACHEL *release one another and look with expressions of happy wonder at the assembled crowd*].

MESHULEM. Good news! Joy! Joy! Glad tidings! Help and deliverance! Where is the Rabbi? Where is Penini? Ah! Here is de Corbeille! And here is Sossen!

VOICES. What's the good news? — Speak up! Speak up! — Out with it! — The good news!

REB JOSEPH [*enters from the left and makes his way through the crowd*]. Good news? This must surely be one of the tokens of God's favor.

PENINI [*gasps, as if he had suddenly understood something. He goes over to the tree where* HILLEL *and* RACHEL *are standing, so as not to be noticed by the throng. He seizes* RACHEL *by the hand and is fixed to the spot in breathless anticipation of the news*].

MESHULEM [*raises his hand as a sign for silence*]. Be silent, and hear how great is the grace of God. [*The babble subsides.*] Hear, then! King Philip is dead, and the new king invites you all to return. [*There is an outburst of great rejoicing.*]

VOICES. How?! — What? — Praised be the Lord

of the Universe! — [*People embrace themselves for joy.*]

PENINI [*at the beginning of* MESHULEM'*s speech he puts his hand into his bosom, draws a very deep breath, takes out a parchment and passes it quickly to* RACHEL. *He turns his stern gaze upon the people, who are beside themselves with joy, and then raises his eyes to heaven*]. Gok! [God.]

RACHEL [*at the announcement of* MESHULEM'*s message she has suppressed a cry of joy. She takes the parchment and strengthens herself to read it. Soon her eyes open wide with astonishment, and her breath comes faster and faster*].

HILLEL [*he has stepped forward a short distance, to get a better look at the messenger and to observe the crowd. At* MESHULEM'*s joyful news he hastens back to* RACHEL'*s side, happiness beaming from his countenance. But one look at* PENINI, *and* HILLEL'*s joy turns to gravity. Seeing that* RACHEL *is absorbed in her excited reading, he stops and looks at her in questioning suspense*].

LEAH [*comes out of her tent, looks about her, catches sight of* PENINI *and does not remove her glance from him*].

RACHEL [*finishes reading, raises her distended eyes to* PENINI *and looks at him, astounded*].

HILLEL. Rachel, what ails you? What has happened?

RACHEL [*still looking at her father, gasps*]. Hillel, my father foresaw it!

HILLEL. What?!

RACHEL. He beheld it in his vision! God revealed it to him. It's all written down here.

HILLEL [*glancing through the writing*]. Wonderful! [*Meanwhile the excitement of the crowd subsides.*]

VOICES. Sh-h-h! — Silence, there! — Quiet! — Quiet!

AVIGDOR. Come, people, let's have silence! Let's hear the particulars. [*There is a hush.*]

MESHULEM. It happened three days ago, on the third day after you left Illyria. King Philip went out hunting. He saw a stag and spurred his horse after it, full speed. His eyes fixed on the stag, he failed to see a deep ditch in his way. Both horse and rider fell into it and were killed.

THE CROWD. Ah-h-h!

REB JOSEPH. The hand of God!

THE CROWD. God's hand! The hand of God!

MESHULEM. Yes, God's hand! And even the new king, King Louis the Tenth, recognized God's hand in the event, and yesterday dispatched messengers in all directions to call back the Jews that had been driven out. He invites you to return to your homes, where you may dwell henceforth in greatest security, and promises to protect you even as the apple of his eye. [*Hurrahs, embraces and glad cries. Children run about in glee, and mothers, with babes in arms, dance for joy.*]

PENINI [*clasps his hands and shakes them in entreaty toward heaven*].

HILLEL [*to* RACHEL]. Do you see how happy they are? They have already forgotten their quest of the Holy Land.

RACHEL. I'll remind them of it.

HILLEL. What will you say to them? They'll not follow you. They'll return to Illyria.

RACHEL. I am my father's tongue.

REB JOSEPH [*to* MESHULEM]. Where are the king's messengers?

MESHULEM. They're on the way. Naturally they're in

no great hurry. But my great joy spurred on my horse, and he flew as if wings carried him. I gave myself no rest, and kept riding through the whole night. Give me a place to lie down,— anywhere at all,— for I need only to close my eyes and I'll fall fast asleep, happy to have been the first to break the good news to you.

REB JOSEPH. And what will become of those Jews who forsook their faith? You're one of them, aren't you?

MESHULEM. To my great shame! We are fast in the clutches of the Church, and our troubles will only just begin. Outwardly we'll have to remain Christians, and perpetuate the Jewish faith in secret. We were weak, and the harshest punishment is none too great. But despite all, we are Jews! We are Jews!

SOSSEN. A wise man once told me a good one. There are three kinds of water, he said, that are used to no purpose: the water that falls into the ocean,— for the ocean has water aplenty; the water that is poured into wine,— for it serves merely to spoil the taste; and the water with which they baptize a Jew — for he remains a Jew despite everything. [*Loud laughter.*]

MESHULEM [*joining in the laughter, then seriously*]. Oh, but we that forsook our faith will have a hard time of it, harder by far than you ever suffered. We are forbidden, under penalty of being burned at the stake, to have anything to do with unbaptized Jews, and at every step we take we shall be spied upon by people with murder in their hearts. Remember! Keep it secret that I have been among you, unless you want the priests to still their hunger for human flesh with a nice roast Meshulem. My joy at the good news was so great that I didn't let the danger hold me back, and I came flying to you.— But I'm so sleepy I can't stand on my feet. Who'll take me to his tent?

Reb Joseph. Come with me, my son. I want to ask you something before you fall asleep.

Meshulem. I'll be sound asleep before you've finished your questions. [*Goes out towards the right with* Reb Joseph, *but suddenly stops and calls out to the throng.*] I'm so drowsy I came near forgetting one of the principal things. The king promises to provide all the clothing and food you need for a whole year. [*Disappears. There is an outburst of wild glee. People dance and sing, kiss and embrace.*]

Hillel [*softy, to* Rachel]. Rachel, consider . . .

Rachel [*entreatingly*]. Beloved, you promised not to interfere with me.

Hillel. Very well. I'll say nothing. The people themselves will answer you, in clear and unmistakable tones.

Blanche [*dizzy from dancing and turning, observes the* Blind Man *being led by his son and daughter-in-law. She shouts derisively*]. Well, Mr. Blind Man, you see that your Cabbala told a lie!

The Blind Man. You impious woman's mouth, how dare you poke fun at the Cabbala!

Blanche. It told a lie, I say. The sorrows of the Jews are at an end. And the Messiah will not come.

The Blind Man. And who are you, to rejoice that the Messiah will not come?

The Beggar. If you could take one look at her, you'd go blind again.

Blanche. You low-down beggar! You two-legged louse! Hey! [*She begins to dance again.*] An end to all our sorrows now!

The Blind Man. Don't be too sure of that. Little you know how God can make our sorrows greater. Who knows what the king's real intentions are? His father beat our bodies with rods, and the son will sting us with scorpions.

VOICES. Shut his mouth for him! Stop his mouth! [*Harsh hands are laid upon him. His son and daughter-in-law defend him.*]

THE BLIND MAN. The Messiah must come! The Messiah must come! The time is ripe for him!

PENINI [*with firm step advances to the quarreling group and cries out in reproach*]. Ah-h-h! [*There is a sudden hush; the* BLIND MAN *is released. The eyes of the crowd are turned to* PENINI, *and all retreat before his look.*]

RACHEL [*hastens to* PENINI's *side and embraces him lovingly*]. Father, I am at your side.

PENINI [*he seizes her hand with both of his, and closes his eyes, as if he would communicate to her every atom of his strength, and the full power of his thoughts*].

RACHEL [*in a loud voice*]. Jews, have you then forgotten altogether the goal of our journey? [*Silence.*] Have you forgotten that we are waiting here for the ships which will bear us across the sea to our Holy Land? [*Deep silence.*] Do you remember that when I asked you whether you wanted to go to Palestine you all cried out lustily, "We'll go! We'll go!"?

SOSSEN. Not I.

AVIGDOR. Nor I, either.

REB JEHIEL. Neither did I.

VOICES. Nor I — Nor I — Nor I!

BLANCHE. And certainly not I!

THE BEGGAR. I was completely indifferent.

LEVI. And suppose we did! At that time Illyria's gates had closed against us. So instead of taking our chances with a strange country we agreed to go to Palestine, because that is our old home and our Holy Land.

But now . . . the case is different! Illyria opens its gates to us!

HILLEL [*with an ironic laugh*]. There you have it! [RACHEL *shudders.* PENINI *opens his eyes and looks at her with silent power.*]

SOSSEN. I call all this a waste of time. We could have packed our things and been on our way back by now.

AVIGDOR. No, not so fast. We must wait for the king's messengers. There are certain conditions that we must make — we must talk these things over calmly. We mustn't appear to be too eager to return.

THE BEGGAR. I'll be the most stubborn of all. They'll have to get down on their knees and beg me to go back.

REB JEHIEL. And anyway, to-morrow is the Sabbath.

RACHEL [*loudly, as if attempting to drown out her own vacillating thoughts*]. Jews, you must not go back to Illyria!

AVIGDOR [*laughing*]. We must not? That's easily said.

SOSSEN. We must not return, you say, when the king sends us a special invitation?

THE BEGGAR. And promises to provide us with clothes and food for a whole year!

BLANCHE. Ha-ha-ha! Just listen to her! [*A confusion of voices arises.*]

RACHEL [*shouting above the din*]. It is true that the new king calls you back to his realm, but do not forget his Christian subjects, who detest your very presence.

AVIGDOR. The king is their ruler and he promises us all security.

RACHEL. And if the people rise against you, will his promises be able to protect you? Know that the Illyrians hate you and seek your destruction. They hooted you out of the kingdom, cursed you and spat upon you, and only armed force kept them from murdering you.

AVIGDOR. That's just it! That same armed force will again be on our side.

SOSSEN. It was always like that, dear daughter. Even before the exile. Yet all of us, including you and your father, dwelt in Illyria and never thought of leaving it. And if you, or your father, or both of you, or any one else at all had come and spoken to us with the tongue of an angel about the Land of Israel, we should perhaps have given you our respectful attention, but hardly one would have stirred from the spot.

HILLEL [*murmurs*]. He's right!

RACHEL [*shudders. Then, under her father's steady glance, she continues in a broken, faltering voice*]. Jews, Illyria is the scene of most bloody insults committed against you. Will you so soon forget them? Where is your pride?

SOSSEN. Pride? Ah! We have long forgotten to be proud before others — with this yellow patch sewed onto us!

LEVI. Pride? There are feelings stronger far than pride. If your father had insulted you, and had immediately regretted it, would you still adhere stubbornly to your pride, and refuse his hand?

MIRIAM. Pride! And in Illyria my child's grave waits for me!

LEVI. Pride! When we shed tears of blood at parting from Illyria! Pride! When we would gladly have given our lives for a grave in Illyria's soil!

HILLEL [*crying out*]. They're right! They speak truth! Our hearts are full of Illyria. It stirs in our every breath, and we should . . . [*Suddenly stops, and turns away his head.*]

RACHEL [*breathless with astonishment, looks at* HILLEL *with distended eyes*].

PENINI [*with firm command, to* RACHEL]. —peak, my —ongue, —peak! [Speak, my tongue, speak.]

RACHEL [*trying to recall something to her thoughts, and to banish a conflicting purpose. She is at a loss for words*]. Fellow Jews . . . Jews . . . Zion waits . . . Zion waits for you! Your old home, the Holy Land, your mother! . . .

AVIGDOR. Bah! Mere words! Come, Sossen, Reb Jehiel, come. We've got to discuss what to say to the king's messengers. [AVIGDOR, SOSSEN *and* REB JEHIEL *walk off to the right, followed by several of the men.*]

LEVI. Come, all of us. Let's await the king's emissaries along the roads. [*Disappears to the left. The crowd follows him, shouting and hurrahing.*]

THE BEGGAR. Well, I'm off to business. Friday is my best day. [*Exit to the left.*]

RACHEL [*calling after the crowd*]. Jews, Zion begs you . . . [*Falls upon* PENINI'S *shoulder.*] Father, I can do no more! Father, they will go back to Illyria!

PENINI [*gasping with despair*]. Oh! —o —ow —I —am —umb! [Now I am dumb!] [*Beats his gaping mouth with his closed fists; closes his mouth and strikes his compressed lips. He throws his arms wildly about, and utters a stifled, long-drawn groan.*]

RACHEL [*wailing*]. Don't, father! Don't! Be patient with me!

PENINI. —o —ow —I am —umb! Gok! [God!] [*Falls upon his face, sobbing bitterly.*]

RACHEL [*kneeling down over him*]. Father! Father!

HILLEL [*breathing hard, covers his eyes*].

LEAH [*she has been standing, all this time, in the opening of her tent, her eyes fixed upon* PENINI. *She walks slowly over to him*]. He is suffering. He is weeping.

CURTAIN

ACT III

SCENE. *Same as Act II.*

RACHEL *is still upon her knees, her face buried in her hands.* HILLEL *stands beside her, his hand resting tenderly upon her head.* LEAH *faces* PENINI'S *tent, her eyes fixed upon the entrance. From time to time she looks at* RACHEL, *with an expression of surprise and sympathy.*

HILLEL. Rachel, how long will you stay like this? Calm yourself, pray.
RACHEL [*sobbing*]. Father! Father! Now he is dumb indeed! How my ears burn! How my heart is torn with grief! I, not the king, rendered him dumb! I, not the king, cut out his tongue!
HILLEL. They didn't care to hear you. They ran off. Even your father could have had no better effect upon them.
RACHEL. No, no,— I know the reason! I did not do my duty. Words came from my mouth, but my head and my heart were elsewhere. How should they be expected to listen to me, when I did not listen to myself? — when I myself heard only you, and my heart was filled with a new fear,— that you would return to Illyria!
HILLEL. We shall all go back to Illyria. You, too, and your father.
RACHEL. We must not think of returning to Illyria! We must go on to Zion!

HILLEL. But you heard the answer of the people.

RACHEL. No, I was not myself when I spoke. If not for that new fear, I would have spoken far differently.

HILLEL. But with the same outcome. Sossen spoke truly when he told you that not even the tongues of angels could have won them away from Illyria.

RACHEL. And will you, too, go back?

HILLEL. Yes, and you, too, with your father.

RACHEL. Impossible! Impossible! Illyria,— the land that maimed him for life!

HILLEL. Do you know — you have no further right to speak to the people in favor of Zion and against Illyria.

RACHEL [*looking up at him in astonishment*]. What can you mean?

HILLEL. Because your words reflect only the indignities they heaped upon your father.

RACHEL. That is not true! That has nothing to do with the glorious thought of Zion: the Zionist ideal is our family heritage.

HILLEL. Then you are determined never to return to Illyria?

RACHEL [*shaking her head*]. They maimed my father there for life.

HILLEL. That might have happened to him in the land of Israel, and under a Jewish king. Would you, in that case, have forsaken the Holy Land, too? And if we had not been driven out, would you have willingly abandoned Illyria through indignation at the king's cruelty? Do you not really love Illyria? Come, let's sit in the shade of this tree, and let me remind you of that beautiful land. Lake and hill, field and forest, I'll recall to your memory. Illyria's spacious skies, Illyria's sun and stars. I'll lead you through all its beloved spots, where we roamed in happy childhood. . . . I'll take you to the graveyard . . . [RACHEL *begins to weep.*] Come, beloved, don't close your heart to me. Let me win you over.

RACHEL [*brokenly*]. And what if my father clings to Zion despite all?

HILLEL. You mean he would go thither, alone? That would amount to abdicating his mission as the Messiah, and you would no longer be his tongue.

RACHEL [*covering her face*]. Terrible! [*Stands thus for a moment, then takes her hands from her eyes.*] But what if my father really *is* the Messiah?

LEAH [*startled. She looks in fright at* RACHEL, *then resumes her fixed gaze upon the entrance to* PENINI'S *tent*].

HILLEL. If your father is really the Messiah, then God's will shall be done. But God will first make his will clear as crystal to us. The day of His miracles is not yet past.

RACHEL. But only just now you said that even the Messiah himself . . .

LEAH [*with a sudden cry, her eyes distended and her arms shielding herself, steps backward to her tent. Then she sinks to her knees and begins to mumble.* RACHEL *springs to her feet in fright*].

HILLEL [*hastening to his mother's side*]. What's the matter, mother? What frightened you so? [*Places his arms about her, nestles her head against him, and caresses her soothingly.*]

PENINI [*comes out of his tent. Looks about for* LEAH, *who is hidden from him by* HILLEL *and* RACHEL. *He gazes upon* RACHEL *with sorrow in his eyes, and shakes his head.— Suddenly, from the left, comes the noise of many people rushing hither and thither.* PENINI *takes a few steps towards the road*].

Leah [*catches sight of him and cries out as before.* Hillel *and* Rachel *follow the direction of* Leah's *glance*].

Rachel. It's my father! Just see with what terror she looks at him!

Hillel. I can't understand it!

Voices [*from the left*]. The king's messengers! The king's messengers! [*The cries and the bustling of people grow louder, as if approaching.*]

Hillel [*trembling, seizes* Rachel's *hand*]. What's all the shouting about? Do I hear rightly? The king's messengers?

Rachel. Now — now something must happen.

Penini [*climbs to the top of the cliff, places himself behind the tree, from where he looks down towards the left. Soon he turns his gaze in the direction of the ocean, and stands thus as if under a spell.*— Avigdor, Sossen, Reb Jehiel *and several other men hasten across the stage from the right to the left. They are stopped by the crowd that has come running in from the other direction*].

Voices. The king's messengers! Messengers from the king!

Levi. I saw them the moment they came dashing out from between the hills.

Avigdor. Silence! Back to your tents! Some of you, if you want to, may sit down by the seashore, but don't look around.

Sossen. I can't see your point.

Avigdor. They mustn't know that we've been waiting here for their arrival, or that we know the news they bring.

Sossen. They needn't know. Can't we all be gathered here for any number of reasons? Let them imagine we're praying.

AVIGDOR. Very well. You can all remain here, then. But remember this: receive their proclamation as coldly as possible. No hurrahs. No shouts of joy.

LEVI. And why all this?

AVIGDOR. That's diplomacy.

THE BEGGAR. It's a game of you urge me and I pretend to refuse. Just as if I were invited to a rich banquet, and I declined absolutely to accept . . . [*A trumpet sounds from the left. The crowd rushes towards the sound.*]

AVIGDOR. Don't run! Don't run!

SOSSEN. Not run, when the trumpet calls us? Why, to stay here now would show that it was all planned beforehand.

AVIGDOR [*with a gesture of scorn*]. Bah!

THE BEGGAR [*shrugging his shoulders*]. Bah!

REB JOSEPH [*enters from the right*]. What's the trumpeting about? Meshulem is sleeping, and I was absorbed in a very deep problem, when . . .

AVIGDOR. The king's messengers are coming.

REB JOSEPH. Then I can go back to my work. What are they to me? I'll not return to Illyria. Christian is Christian, and Jew is Jew; they'll never cease their persecution of us.

AVIGDOR [*impatiently*]. Yes, yes. I know your notions well.

REB JOSEPH. A pity you don't share them. Yes, I'm going right back to my work. And I rejoice that I'll soon be in a country where I can have my holy Talmud once again. Oh, it will be like a light breaking through the darkness. You can't imagine how useful the volume on Idolatry would be for this problem that I'm working on now. It's about a priest who became a Christian and then returned to the Jewish faith.— A weighty matter. [*Exit to the right. As he goes out, the crowd comes flocking back to the stage from the left. Then comes* COUNT DE GUESCLIN, *followed by a trumpeter. The* COUNT *holds in his hand a parchment scroll. The trumpeter holds his trumpet in his right hand, and in his left a rolled-up document. He stands several steps behind the* COUNT, *and prevents the people from approaching too near to his master. The crowd forms a semicircle about them.* AVIGDOR, SOSSEN *and* REB JEHIEL *stand at the rear.* HILLEL *and* RACHEL, *tense with excitement, take up their position near* AVIGDOR'S *tent.* LEAH *steals away from the crowd towards the cliff, and stops not far from* PENINI.]

HILLEL [*watching* LEAH]. I can't understand it!

THE TRUMPETER [*raises his instrument to his lips and sounds three flourishes*].

COUNT DE GUESCLIN [*when the sounds of the trumpet have died away*]. My Jewish friends, I come to you with great news.

THE BEGGAR [*sighing*]. Yes. Indeed.

VOICES. Sh! Quiet!

COUNT DE GUESCLIN. King Philip is dead.... [*Pauses, so as to see what effect this news has upon his hearers. The crowd is unmoved; not a sound is uttered.*] He met with an accident while out hunting and died.... [*Pauses again.*]

THE BEGGAR. Blessed be the Righteous Judge!

BLANCHE [*bursting into tears*]. The handsome king!

A GROUP OF CHILDREN [*begin to sing and dance in a ring*]. Tra-la-la! Tra-la-la! [*They are quickly hushed by some of their elders.*]

COUNT DE GUESCLIN [*smiling indulgently*]. Children

can't hide their feelings. . . . Dance, my little ones, and make your fathers and mothers dance with you. There's no reason for you to bemoan King Philip's death. Dance with all the more zest because his son, the noble Crown Prince Louis, succeeds him to the throne.

THE CHILDREN [*resume their dancing*]. Tra-la-la! Tra-la-la! The king is calling us back to Illyria!

VOICES. Hush! Hush!

COUNT DE GUESCLIN. What! The children know it? Then they've spared me the trouble of telling it to you. Yes, King Louis calls you all back to Illyria.

THE CHILDREN [*dancing*]. Tra-la-la! Tra-la-la! The King calls us back to Il-lyr-i-a! [*The crowd greets his words without a sound or a motion.*]

COUNT DE GUESCLIN. What? You are silent? You don't jump for joy? You stand unmoved and don't join your children in their dance? Perhaps you don't believe me? Here, here is the king's proclamation to you, signed by himself and sealed with his signet-ring. [*Motions to his trumpeter, who blows three times, as before. The* COUNT *after the sounds of the trumpet have died away, reads in a loud voice.*]

"I, Louis the Tenth, by the grace of God King of Illyria, to you, my Jewish subjects: It was the will of God to call unto Himself my lamented father, King Philip the Fourth, and to place me upon his throne. And because I was never in accord with my father of blessed memory in his decree that you be driven forth beyond the borders of our beloved Illyria, I hasten, as soon as God has placed the scepter in my hand, to revoke this harsh and unjust decree."

[*Pauses and looks upon the faces of his hearers.*]

THE CROWD [*stands motionless, as if petrified*].

Act III]   THE DUMB MESSIAH

Count de Guesclin [*shrugs his shoulders and continues to read, as if counting each word*].

"You are welcome to be my subjects, and the gates of Illyria are open to you, with every privilege you formerly enjoyed. . . ." [*Murmurs of happiness from the crowd.*]

Blanche. The gracious king!

The Beggar. — The privilege, for example, of wearing a yellow patch.

Count de Guesclin [*looks sternly in the direction of* The Beggar's *voice*].

Voices. Shh! None of that!

Count de Guesclin [*resuming his reading*].

"With every privilege you formerly enjoyed. . . ."

The Beggar. I've heard that already.

Voices. Shh! Quiet! The impudence of the man!

Count de Guesclin.

"You will give me your oath of allegiance, and I know that I shall have in you most loyal subjects. On my side you have my royal promise that I will give to you and your children and all your property my royal protection, so long as the Lord grants me to reign over my realm. As proof of my good will towards you, know that one of my first acts was to punish the ministers who led my father astray by their evil counsel against you, and I have made provision to support those of you who have suffered most from the decree of exile with food and clothing for a whole year. Subscribed to by my own hand and sealed with the royal seal." [*With fervor.*]

"Louis the Tenth, King of Illyria." [*Looks about him. The crowd stand unmoved, as before. By this time* Count de Guesclin *is thoroughly astonished.*] What? You still say nothing? No shouts of joy, no

glad outcry, no faces beaming with happiness? —
Where are your leaders? Where is the noble Penini?
Is the poor man ill, perhaps? — Where is the Rabbi?
[AVIGDOR, SOSSEN *and* REB JEHIEL *push their way
through the crowd and come before the* COUNT.]
Ah, here comes Monsieur de Corbeille. Greetings,
friend!

AVIGDOR [*bowing*]. Greetings, noble Count de Guesclin!

COUNT DE GUESCLIN. You can tell me, perhaps, why
you all receive my news so coldly. Are you not happy
at the king's favor? Are you not glad to return to
Illyria? Or do you still hesitate to believe me? Here,
take the document; read it yourself and be assured.
[*Hands the parchment to* AVIGDOR.]

AVIGDOR [*acknowledges the parchment with a bow*].
We have not yet recovered from our fright, noble Count.

COUNT DE GUESCLIN. Yes, yes. I can understand
that. Yet —

AVIGDOR. And we must discuss the proposal.

COUNT DE GUESCLIN. Discuss it? Then you have already discovered a new home?

AVIGDOR. We have re-discovered our old one.

RACHEL [*softly*]. Hillel, do you hear?

HILLEL. Diplomacy. Nothing more.

COUNT DE GUESCLIN [*looking sharply at* AVIGDOR,
and trying to understand]. I don't understand your
words.

AVIGDOR. Not always have we been dwellers in
strange lands, noble Count. Not always have we been in
exile. Long, long ago Israel had its own land.

COUNT DE GUESCLIN. Is Illyria, then, a strange land
to you?

AVIGDOR. We were driven from Illyria like strangers.

COUNT DE GUESCLIN. The same thing happened to you in your ancient land.

AVIGDOR. But then we were conquered in man-to-man conflict; Illyria kicked us out as if we were nothing but dogs.

RACHEL [*as before*]. Doesn't he speak the truth, Hillel?

HILLEL. And yet . . .

COUNT DE GUESCLIN. Yes, it was a grievous wrong against you. But now the king desires to right that wrong. How deep that desire is you may judge when I tell you that he has sent you horses and wagons.

VOICES [*with glad shout*]. Horses and wagons?!

COUNT DE GUESCLIN. Yes, horses and wagons, to lighten your homeward return. [*A great stir among the people. Shouts of joy.— The people have forgotten their rôle. The children begin to dance and the older folk join them.*]

HILLEL [*to* RACHEL]. There! Do you see now?

COUNT DE GUESCLIN. At last! The horses and wagons have overridden all your objections. Or do you want to deliberate further?

THE BEGGAR [*in a low voice, to* AVIGDOR]. Horses and wagons and diplomacy!

AVIGDOR. The voice of the people is the voice of God. Blessed be the Lord and our gracious king, henceforth and forever. [*The people's rejoicing increases.*] But we must— [AVIGDOR, SOSSEN, REB JEHIEL, COUNT DE GUESCLIN *and several other men step aside to the left and engage in earnest conversation.*]

PENINI [*gazes at the dancing, bustling crowd, then towards* RACHEL, *and begins to descend the cliff*].

RACHEL [*to* HILLEL]. My father has something to say to the people! His eyes are calling me! Hillel!

HILLEL. Wait. Let him tell you what he wants. But you see the people — words will accomplish nothing. Only a miracle can move them now.

PENINI [*he has reached the bottom of the cliff. The crowd notices him, and there is a sudden hush. All eyes are turned upon him, and people make way for him in deep respect. He walks slowly, solemnly, his gaze fixed upon* RACHEL].

LEAH [*soon appears a few paces behind* PENINI].

COUNT DE GUESCLIN. This is the noble Penini.— Heavens! How they have disfigured him! [*Approaches* PENINI.] Poor, unfortunate friend, accept my greetings. [*Offers* PENINI *his hand.*]

PENINI [*refuses to notice him and walks on*].

COUNT DE GUESCLIN [*looks around, seeking an explanation for the rebuff*]. How now? What can this mean? — Here Menahem Penini, I have a letter of pardon from the king. [*Takes the parchment from the trumpeter.*]

THE BEGGAR. And where's a note from the king for me?

VOICES. Sh-h! Quiet! Shut his mouth for him!

COUNT DE GUESCLIN [*offering the document to* PENINI]. He cannot restore your tongue to you, nor can he wipe out the memory of your sufferings, but . . .

PENINI [*looks at him blankly, takes the parchment, crumples it up, throws it to the ground and walks on*].

VOICES. Oh! The letter! The royal letter!

COUNT DE GUESCLIN. The king's letter! — You are ill. That will be your excuse. Well, I have delivered my message and now I can ride back to the Court. Good-by to all of you. [*He motions to the trumpeter, and both go off to the left.*]

AVIGDOR [*following him*]. Let not the act of one who has suffered so terribly be set against us. [*There is a great commotion. Cries of woe. Wringing of hands. Al pursue* COUNT DE GUESCLIN.]

PENINI [*goes over to* RACHEL, *looks at her mutely, penetratingly*].

RACHEL [*at a loss*]. Father! What — shall — I — do?

PENINI. — peak! [Speak.]

RACHEL [*despairingly*]. I don't know what to say! My heart is heavy, my mind is in confusion — Father, they will all return to Illyria.

PENINI [*nodding towards* HILLEL]. He!

RACHEL [*softly, embarrassed*]. Words will do nothing. Only a miracle can help!

PENINI [*takes from a pocket a parchment and gives it to her*].

RACHEL [*takes it with trembling hands and looks through it*]. I am to tell them your dreams,— your visions? Will they believe me?

PENINI [*sternly, snatching the parchment from her*]. -ot be-ieve me?! [AVIGDOR, *followed by the people, returns.*]

AVIGDOR [*angrily, to* PENINI]. What did you do that for? Do you want to pull down the wrath of the king upon us?

PENINI [*continues to gaze sternly upon* RACHEL].

SOSSEN. The idea! To insult the word of a king! That's forbidden even in the Scriptures.

REB JEHIEL. And right before the eyes of the Count!

VOICES. Oh! Oh! For shame!

AVIGDOR. He left in great wrath, red with anger.

VOICES. Woe is us! Woe is us!

AVIGDOR. You want to force us to follow you?

PENINI [*nods "yes" emphatically. Cries out loudly*]. — es! [Yes.]

AVIGDOR [*furious*]. What! You would force us, would you? How dare you presume such a thing! Are you appointed by God?

PENINI [*as before*]. — es!

AVIGDOR. What? You dare say yes? Would you have us believe that you're the Messiah?

PENINI [*with a slow, firm gesture he gives his parchment to* AVIGDOR].

LEAH [*with a sudden outcry*]. He is the Messiah! [*Several women scream in fright.*]

PENINI [*shudders, takes a step forward and raises his eyes to heaven*]. Go-ok! [God!]

AVIGDOR [*gapes in stupefaction*].

THE BLIND MAN [*with a cry of terror*]. Who speaks there? Who made that cry?

RACHEL [*seizing* HILLEL'S *arm with both hands*]. A miracle, Hillel! A miracle!

LEAH [*louder than before*]. He is the Messiah! [*The people recoil from* PENINI. *The women and the children begin to cry.*]

THE BLIND MAN [*as before*]. Through whom has God revealed this to us?

VOICES. The mad woman! The crazy woman!

RACHEL [*with a cry of exaltation*]. God speaks to us through a wandering spirit!

HILLEL [*as if to himself*]. A miracle! A miracle!

LEAH. He is the Messiah!

THE BLIND MAN [*ecstatically*]. Oh, to be able to see once again! I want to look upon him! Great God, I want to look upon your Messiah! Give me my eyes! Let me have my sight again! [*Sinks to his knees. The people, inspired by him, likewise fall upon their knees.*]

BLANCHE [*becomes hysterical. She tears her hair and beats her breasts.* THE BEGGAR *kneels.* AVIGDOR, SOSSEN *and* REB JEHIEL *are at the left.* RACHEL *and* HILLEL *to the right.* LEAH *at the rear*].

PENINI [*raises his hands to Heaven and utters cries whose joy is mingled with tears*].

RACHEL [*agitated, confused*]. God speaks to us through a wandering spirit! The Messiah stands here before you! Follow him! Listen, my people! While my father lay in his dungeon, he beheld a vision. As he lay there waiting for death, he heard a voice. It was the voice of God. God revealed Himself to him, to His chosen one. And the Lord said to him . . . [*Stops suddenly as if hypnotized, her eyes staring at* LEAH. *The crowd looks at her in amazement, then follows the direction of her glances.* PENINI *drops his hands and does the same.* LEAH, *her eyes burning with the fire of insanity, begins to go from one person to another.*]

LEAH [*as she walks along*]. The Messiah! The Messiah! The Messiah! . . . [*Stops before the blind man*]. You are the Messiah! You are the Messiah! Ha-ha-ha! . . . You are the Messiah! You are the Messiah!

THE BLIND MAN. Who's poking fun here?

LEAH. Ha-ha-ha! [*To* THE BEGGAR.] *You* are the Messiah! You are the Messiah!

THE BEGGAR. What? Now it's I?

LEAH. *You, you, you.* . . . [*The people begin to rise from their knees.*]

THE BEGGAR. And who else is Messiah? [*Pointing to* BLANCHE.] She, perhaps?

LEAH. She, she, she. . . . She is the Messiah! [*There is an explosion of laughter.*] Ha-ha-ha. . . .

[*She begins to dance in a circle.*] The Messiah! The Messiah! The Messiah!

PENINI [*turns his gaze to* RACHEL].

RACHEL [*going over to* HILLEL, *and leaning her head upon his shoulders. She is crushed*]. The miracle has vanished. They're laughing. I'll speak no more.

PENINI [*clutches his throat as if he were choking. He utters several shrieks of deep despair, and suddenly, with a cry of "Go-ok!"* [*God!*] *he makes a dash to the cliff, runs to the top, and from there throws himself into the sea*].

RACHEL [*horror-struck, advancing a few steps*]. Father! [*Falls into* HILLEL's *arms. The crowd look with terror into the sea where* PENINI *has disappeared.*]

LEAH [*still dancing*]. The Messiah! The Messiah! The Messiah!

SLOW CURTAIN

AUTHOR'S NOTES TO "THE DUMB MESSIAH"

The Characters, the Plot and the Country

All the persons of my drama are imaginary figures,— children of my fancy. This is true likewise of the whole story of the dumb Messiah.

By the words " in the time of a great expulsion of the Jews," however, is meant the banishment of all Jews from France in the year 1306, during the reign of Philip IV, known also as Philip the Fair; but since the action never took place in France, and the characters never dwelt in that country, I chose as background the land of Illyria, where many poets before me have set the children of their fancy.

The Expulsion and the Return in History

I

(See " History of the Jews," * by Professor H. Graetz, Vol. IV, Chapter II, pages 46–53.)

" Philip IV, le Bel, at that time the king of France, suddenly issued a secret order (21st June, 1306) imposing the strictest silence, to the higher and lower officials throughout the kingdom, to put all the Jews of France under arrest on one and the same day, without warning of any kind. Before the Jews had fully recov-

---

* I have given the author's references to Graetz in the language of the English version, interpolating a few passages which do not occur in that translation.— Tr.

ered from fasting on the Day of Lamentation in remembrance of the destruction of Jerusalem, and as they were about to begin their daily business, the constables and jailers appeared, laid hands upon them, and dragged young and old, women and children, to prison. (10th Ab —— 22nd July.) There they were told that they had to quit the country within the space of a month, leaving behind their goods and the debts owing to them. Whoever was found in France after that time was liable to the penalty of death. . . . The king wanted to replenish his coffers from the property of the Jews. . . . That he aimed at the possessions of the Jews was shown by his relentless plundering. The officials left the unhappy Jews nothing beyond the clothes they wore, and to every one, no matter how wealthy he had previously been, not more than seemed necessary for a day's living. (12 gros Tournois.) Wagonfuls of the property of the Jews, gold, silver and precious stones, were transported to the king; and less valuable objects were sold at a ridiculously low price.

". . . The expatriated Jews dispersed in all parts of the world; many traveled to Palestine. But the majority remained as near as possible to the French borders. . . . Their intention was to wait for a favorable change of fortune which would put an end to their dispersion and permit them to return to the land of their birth. . . .

". . . Louis X had recalled them nine years after their banishment (1315). The king, himself seized by a desire to abrogate the ordinances of his father and indict his counsellors, had been solicited by the people and the nobility, who could not do without the Jews, to readmit them into France. He accordingly entered into negotiations with them in reference to their return. But the

Jews did not accept his proposal without deliberation, for they well knew the inconstancy of the French kings, and the fanatical hatred of the clergymen against them. They hesitated at first, and then submitted their conditions."

II

(From the book "Shebet Jehuda," chapters 21 and 24.)

"In the year 5046 of the creation of the world there ascended to the throne a cruel monarch called Philip, son of Philip. He banished all the Jews from his kingdom, treating them with extreme cruelty, despoiling them of their silver and gold and all other property of whatever nature, so that they were cast forth robbed of everything. . . .

"In the year 5055 that same king Philip who had banished them went hunting and beheld a stag running before him. He gave chase upon horseback, galloping at full speed. There lay in his path, however, a deep ditch, into which fell both he and his horse; he broke his neck and died, and all men knew that his cruelty to the Jews had been the cause of his death. . . . To this terrible king there succeeded his son, who proved to be a good-hearted ruler, and a lover of justice and righteousness. When he saw the fate that had overtaken his father he sent a messenger to the Jews with an invitation to return to their cities in the utmost confidence; he promised to guard them as the apple of his eye. . . . 'But,' questioned some among the Jews, 'even if the king promises security, how shall we be able to defend ourselves if the people should rise against us?' . . . After a short while, however, they returned, saying, 'Let us go back to the land of our birth, for she is our motherland, and the king is a good and just ruler, and that which he promises he keeps.' And thus they returned to their provinces. On the way, however, they were befallen by highwaymen and robbed. . . . Whereupon the king ordered the Jews to be provided with clothes and food for an entire year. . . ."

A Few Historical Details

(See Graetz, *op. cit.*, Vol. IV, Chap. XI, pages 352–353.)

". . . The graves of their forefathers were dearer to them than all besides, and from these they found parting hardest. The thought of these graves filled them with deepest grief. . . . The Jews of Segovia assembled three days before their exodus around the graves of their forefathers. . . . They tore up many of the tombstones to bear them away as memorial relics. . . . Many rabbis permitted women and children to sing, and caused pipers and drummers to go before, making lively music, so that for a while the wanderers should forget their gnawing grief."

www.ingramcontent.com/pod-product-compliance
Lightning Source LLC
Chambersburg PA
CBHW032107090426
42743CB00007B/271